CRAFTING CONNECTION

Transform how you communicate with
yourself and others

FELICITY DWYER

First published in Great Britain by Practical Inspiration Publishing, 2022

ISBN   9781788604017   (print)
       9781788604031   (epub)
       9781788604024   (mobi)

Want to bulk-buy copies of this book for your team and colleagues? We can introduce case studies, customize the content and co-brand *Crafting Connection* to suit your business's needs.

Please email info@practicalinspiration.com for more details.

Practical Inspiration
Publishing

Appreciation for *Crafting Connection*

Crafting Connection is a must-read guide to communication and building better relationships. Felicity shares her deep experience and expertise through her versatile '3-D' model, crafting connections on three levels: with oneself, with others, and as a community. Packed full of insights and examples, each chapter satisfies the head (through reasoned logic and evidence-based science), the heart (impactful outcomes, reflective questions), and the hands (practical guidance and activities). Highly recommended to anyone who wants to consider how they communicate and connect, whether at home, at work, or in their wider community.

Jess Annison, OBE
Jess Annison Coaching

Crafting Connection is excellent. It is very accessible and easy to read. The ideas are clearly explained, and the book gives useful and accessible tools and techniques. Felicity's presence is just right; she shares her stories and experiences with a flavour and personality that is authentic. The concepts are valid and cogent and shared with a light touch so that it doesn't overwhelm or interfere. It's thought-provoking, yet not too highbrow or complex. A sensible book for sensible people. This stuff matters, and true connection with self and with others can be life-changing.

Krista Powell Edwards, BA Hons (Open)
MA PgDipPM Chartered FCIPD
Author of *Credible HR: The Handbook for People Professionals to Communicate with Influence and Impact*

I found this book fascinating to read.

Felicity does a wonderful job of sharing her extensive knowledge of effective communication and progressively helped me understand how to connect better with those I meet.

To fully appreciate her advice and recommendations I will read it again – and look forward to doing so.

Jeremy Glyn
Author of *Achieving Happiness is 'Easy as ABC'*

I found *Crafting Connection* to be an elegant, accessible, and practical guide to creating a more meaningful, authentic life by deepening the connection you have with yourself and with others.

I really liked the Connecting in 3D framework as it makes sense of a big topic, and because it's simple, it's both powerful and memorable. Once you see communication and connection through the Connecting in 3D lens, you can't unsee it in your daily life!

The book is packed with loads of simple, easy-to-action tools. Felicity draws on a multitude of therapies and disciplines, and there is so much wisdom in *Crafting Connection* that even adopting a fraction of the recommendations in the book could be life-changing.

This book could help many people and I would highly recommend it.

Sarah Grant
Nutritional therapist and wellbeing coach, Gut Reaction

I really enjoyed this book; it is eminently readable. It combines intellectually sound theories with relatable stories to bring them to life.

I especially liked the exercises that allowed me to apply the lessons in the course of my reading so that I finished the book with good retention of what I had read (I don't find this with every book I read).

I like the structure of the book, which leads us from connecting with ourselves, then others, and finally building a community. Felicity introduces fresh ideas to some established thinking in a way that connects the dots of effective communication for life.

Glenda Shawley
MD, Fabulous Networking

Wow, this has hit the spot very successfully. As a trainer, facilitator, coach, and counsellor myself there are many open questions in my toolbox and I love asking them of others to obtain full answers. Felicity has used appropriate questions with me in this publication. She has really caused me to think about how I communicate and connect with myself and others. This easy-to-read and understand book takes the reader on a journey about inter- and intra-communication, which will be new to many and a revision for others.

Graham Le-Gall – author
Galleou Public Speaking and creator of
The Peas of Public Speaking®

I've really enjoyed this book. I found the themes to be much deeper than I had expected, and immersed myself in all the chapters and practices throughout. There were so many thoughts and concepts that I enjoyed exploring; reading the book has had a very positive impact on me. I will definitely be recommending it to my Mindset Bookclub!

Angela Marshall
Travel Counsellor

Felicity Dwyer has the rare gifts of combining emotional acuity with practical solutions to the basic human problems of connecting and relationships.

Her invaluable book, which is based on personal experience and lifelong learning, deserves to be widely read.

Nick Keith
Author of *Feel it as a Man: A Fool's Guide to Relationships*

This book could not be better timed for our shouty, social media driven world where communication is often downgraded to scoring points and provoking reactions. Felicity provides a clear and insightful guide to what good communication should be. Connecting in 3D is a powerful building block which we can all benefit from using in every area of our lives. Highly recommended.

Liz Gresson
Organising Expert at All Organised for You

To my father Christopher Dwyer who taught me the value of lifelong learning, the power of unconditional love, and that it's never too late to write a book!

Contents

Welcome to
Crafting Connection

Think about a conversation that had a powerful impact on you. A conversation where you really felt heard. A conversation where you felt you learnt something about the other person's inner world and worldview. A conversation where you changed your mind about something. A conversation where something you said sparked ideas and thinking for another person, or group of people…

What difference did this conversation make to you?

Communicating and connecting with others in a meaningful way is life enhancing. And the ability to do this well is also a practical skill, a craft. At work, we may find creative ideas through a lively brainstorming session; we may grasp a sense of our potential through a thought-provoking coaching conversation; we may feel a glow from a friendly chat with a colleague. And we may experience the value day-to-day of clear communication about what's expected from us, and what we expect from others. In contrast, we may experience what we perceive as negativity, hostility, and criticism at work, and long for a different way of relating.

In our personal relationships, we may seek excitement or challenge, or we may yearn for easy and comfortable everyday communication. We are likely to want our close friendships, and romantic relationships, to meet some of our needs for depth of connection. Yet no one person, even a life partner, can meet all our needs. A good network of family, friends, and communities provides the tapestry of support and stimulation that is essential for good emotional health.

The skills that help us communicate and connect are some of the most important ones that we will ever learn and use: at home, at work, and in our social interactions. Time spent on growing and building our ability and flair in these areas will be richly rewarded in terms of our relationships, our career prospects, and our personal development.

Connecting Within

When thinking about the way you relate to others, it's helpful to think first about how you connect with yourself. A relationship you'll have throughout your life is with the person you were, the person you are now, and the person you will be in the future. Building a good relationship with that person, by learning to accept and appreciate yourself will help you connect more deeply with other people. I'm calling this level Connecting Within, and it's where the exploration in this book starts.

Connecting Within is not about being self-absorbed or self-obsessed. It's the opposite. Because the better you know yourself, the more likely you are to be able to separate your reality from that of another person.

And yes, we all live in separate realities. By this, I don't mean there's no external objective reality with which we interact. Instead, I mean that your experience of life is always mediated by the interplay between the external world and the physical make-up of your being. The latter includes your senses, through which you take in information, as well as your nervous system and neural networks. Your subjective experience will be affected by a myriad of factors, including your physical health on any given day, and the balance of hormones and neurotransmitters circulating around your body and brain.

Connecting With

We share a common biological inheritance with all human beings. Yet no two people will ever have exactly the same life experiences or have developed identical interconnections between the neurons in their brains. Understanding our uniqueness can lead to a sense of curiosity and enquiry into how we see the world, as we can both appreciate ourselves and understand that ours is not the only way of seeing. This can help us to communicate our perspective as truthfully as we can, whilst also being open to the perspectives of others.

The differences between us can make other human beings endlessly fascinating. Developing the ability to really listen to other people is the starting point for understanding. It opens a channel of communication which allows us to build a depth of connection with others. In this book, we'll explore different ways to connect and communicate with other people, personally and professionally.

Connecting Beyond

And there is another level of connection, which goes beyond one-to-one or small group conversations. We are connected to the planet on which we live. We are literally made of the same stuff as the Earth. We are carbon-based life-forms; our bodies hold trace metals and minerals from the Earth. We exchange molecules and atoms with the atmosphere, with plants, with other animals. We transform energy from one form into another (in this case the energy from food powers the movement of my fingers on the keyboard).

In connecting with other people, it can be helpful to remember that we are all part of something larger. That may be a geographical community – everyone in our household, street, town, or nation state. It may be a community of interest – for example, I feel connected to fellow coaches and facilitators around the world. It may be a workplace community, or the community of people connected with a pastime such as sport or the theatre, or involvement in a political or social cause.

Connecting in 3D

This book is structured around these three dimensions of connection: Connecting Within; Connecting With; Connecting Beyond. I'm calling this structure *Connecting in 3D*.

Our connections form ever-changing patterns, like threads moving around one another in the deft hands of a lacemaker. There are threads of words, body language, and tone of voice, constantly shifting and changing, making new patterns. There are words and the depth of meaning beneath the words. And there are all the associations the words have for you, and all the associations the words have for me. There's also the images you see, and the images I see. You may see the word *vessel* as a beautiful Greek urn and I may see a vessel as a sailing ship, and our words meet and dance, or collide.

You are always at the centre of your own circle, as illustrated in the diagram on page 6. From this place you interact with other people and the environment in which you find your-self. Different people and different interactions form infinitely varied patterns. It's like turning the drum of a kaleidoscope and seeing the images and dynamics shift. Interactions are never exactly the same, yet sometimes you may find yourself caught up in a way of relating that is grindingly familiar.

There's always part of the pattern of interaction that's in your power to change, which is in what you say and how you behave. And when you make changes from the inside out, they are more powerful. Hence the starting point is the connection and integration taking place within yourself.

As I know from experience, the benefits of this increased connection show up in all areas of life, and in both personal and professional relationships. You may find yourself becoming more confident in speaking out, because you're connected with what really matters to you. You'll build strong relationships by being better able to understand other people. It can help you to make wise decisions by connecting with what is right for you. It can help your career by developing your leadership skills, your creative thinking skills, your networking skills, and your ability to work and communicate effectively with people who may be very different to you.

The ideas you'll find in this book are offered in the spirit of a conversation. You'll discover different ways of thinking about the way we connect with ourselves and others. There are also a range of practices which I've found helpful in making meaning in my life. I invite you try out some of these practices and experience them for yourself. And there are questions for you to reflect on, in the spirit of a dialogue.

I'll be interested to hear your thoughts that emerge as you read, you can contact me via my website; details are on page 222. I've also put together a *Connection Craft Kit* for you, packed with resources related to the ideas in this book. See page 212 for information.

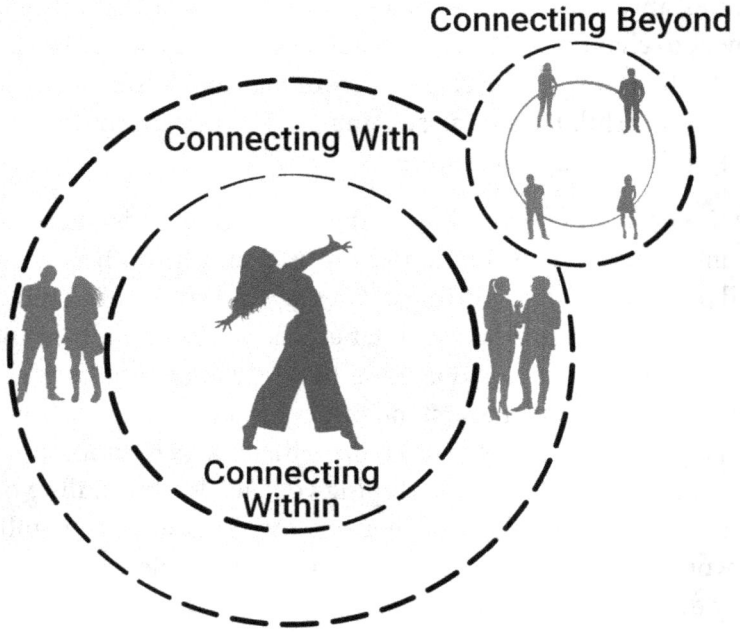

Connecting Beyond

Connecting With

Connecting Within

Dimension 1

Connecting Within

A school netball pitch. A 13-year-old girl with no interest or aptitude for netball, her mind elsewhere, in an imaginary world which is far more real to her than the physical space in which she stands. The ball comes her way and, in a belated attempt to catch it, she misses and the ball comes down hard on her little finger and fractures it. Not serious, but painful. It's strapped to the next finger while it heals, and – the real silver lining – no more netball for a few weeks!

As that child, I lived very much in my imagination, I wasn't co-ordinated or skilled at physical activities, and would rather be reading a book than playing sports. The experience on the netball court stands out in my memory because of the pain involved, but looking back, I spent much of my time at school with my body in one place and my mind in another. This made it difficult for me to connect effectively with myself or with others.

And now I'm writing a book all about connection and my starting point is about connecting within, by which I mean connecting with different aspects of yourself. This dimension is indicated by the inner circle of the *Connecting in 3D* model. Like many of the concepts and ideas in this book, this sense of connecting within didn't always come naturally to me. It's been developed over the years, through reading, learning from inspirational teachers and, most importantly, through practice. In learning to connect with myself, I've found a gateway to connecting more easily with other people. Because these are learned skills for me,

I also love to share and teach them. I'm confident that, whatever your starting point, you can always expand into an even greater depth of connection, with yourself and others.

A foundation stone for connection is the ability to bring your attention into the present moment in time. We can listen deeply to ourselves (and others) when our attention is grounded in the present, and this is the reason why the first chapter explores the concept of presence.

In my experience, the easiest way to come to the present moment is to connect with physical sensation, in particular the sensation of touch. So, we go on to explore this in Chapter 2, before moving on to consider our values, our thoughts, and our inner landscape in the form of the metaphors and stories that help create our experience of reality.

The bedrock of my work as a facilitator, trainer, and coach is my ability to be fully present with other people. And I'm aware that my presence and impact is much more powerful and transformational when I also feel more connected with myself, in the ways described in this part of the book. The practices in this section are simple, yet powerful, and I hope they will serve you well, as they have me.

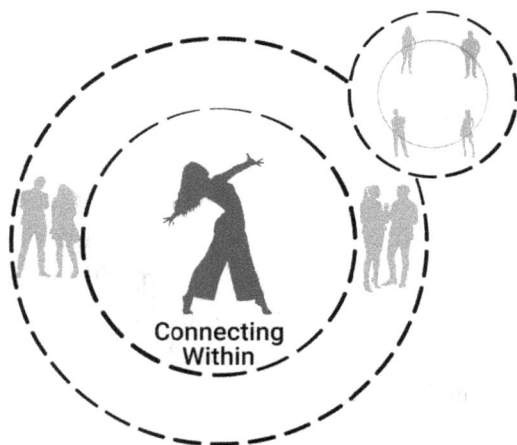

Connecting Within

Chapter 1

It all starts here
Presence as the gateway to connection

Where are you now as you read this book? How much of your attention is fully focused on these words? To what extent are you aware of your body, your surroundings, and your own reactions to what you are reading?

Being present with what is going on right now opens a gateway to connection. It's like a golden key to connecting with other people and to connecting with yourself. It allows you space to notice both what is going on inside yourself and what is happening in your environment. It's difficult to truly connect unless you're able to bring your attention back to the present moment.

It's in the present moment that you can connect with your body, in particular the subtle sensations it offers you, rich with information and wisdom.

It's in the present moment that you connect with the part of yourself that is a still point in time; the part that can observe your own thinking, and which offers you the realization that you're much more than just your thoughts.

It's in the present moment that you can make choices about where to direct your attention. And the quality of your relationship with yourself and others is, to a great extent, determined by where you direct and place your attention.

In this chapter, you'll explore different perspectives on time. And you'll discover practical exercises to help you connect more deeply with the present moment.

You're a time traveller

As a human being, you possess a magical ability to time travel.

You can take yourself back, into your past. You can review and learn from things that have happened. And on the darker side, I'm sure you have the ability at times to infuse your mood with emotions such as regret.

And you can take yourself forwards, into the future. You can visualize and plan, hope and dream. On the darker side, you may sometimes find yourself caught up in thoughts or feelings of anxiety and fear about what might happen.

A superpower for building a connected life is the ability to choose where in time to consciously direct your attention rather than feel caught up in the time travelling. And a starting point for navigating time is to be able to reliably bring yourself back to the present. To the here. And the now.

Where do you reside?

Do you have a sense of how much time you spend in the past, present, or future?

You may have observed people who spend a lot of time in the past. They talk about what has happened to them; good or bad. They may recount conversations that they've been involved in, or continually revisit formative events that took place earlier in their lives.

And others are much more future oriented. They are more likely to talk about what they are going to do and how they see the future. They may make concrete plans, or dream and imagine how the months and years ahead may turn out.

Both perspectives are valuable. Looking back in a reflective way is how we learn from the past. It can help us to make sense of things that have happened to us and then put them in context. When we tell our life stories, we connect events to form a narrative that takes us from the past into the present. This gives us a sense of continuity and connection to our personal histories. It also creates a sense of cause and effect. This can be instructive, but also potentially misleading. We may draw conclusions from an outcome to a situation that isn't justified. For this reason, it's important to remain open to reviewing the meaning we draw from a situation, and to be prepared to challenge our own assumptions about the impact of our past.

Looking ahead is important too, so that we can make plans. We can't be sure about what will happen, as there are always factors outside our control. But we can come up with a vision, strategies and actions that give us the best chance of achieving what we want for ourselves, and for the people and causes we care about. In a leadership role, for example, we need to build a sense of where we, our team, or our organization are heading, so that we can direct our energies in that direction. And in our careers, a sense of our desired future will give us a focus on the skills we need to develop and the opportunities we need to look out for.

But there are downsides to living in the past and future too. Take regret. This is an emotion that can affect us in the present; we may wish we had behaved differently or that our life had turned out in a different way. Yes, it's important to reflect on, and learn from, our experiences. But we cannot change the past. I've learned over the years that the key to peace is to accept things as they are, to learn from mistakes, and to let go. There is more about this in Chapter 4.

And if we live too much in our dreams for the future, we miss out on the juiciness of the present. We may also suffer from anxiety, through imagining problems or catastrophes that may happen in the future.

It certainly makes sense to see potential downsides before making an important decision or when doing a risk assessment. But most of what we imagine could go wrong won't happen in reality. And if it does, we'll have no choice but to deal with it then. It's sensible and responsible to make contingency plans. But don't live your life on the basis that things will turn out badly. Trust that you'll be able to deal with whatever the future brings. And in the meantime, enjoy what's good right now.

So, if we can develop a skill at navigating time perspectives, we can ground ourselves in the present moment and make deliberate choices about when to move our attention forward into the future or back to the past.

The power of being present

I believe that the ability to be present is fundamental to the ideas I share in this book and essential for deep connection.

One strand of my work is facilitating leadership training programmes. On these courses, one of the areas we think about is that of leadership presence. Some people think of leadership presence as a kind of special power or gravitas that charismatic leaders possess. But what it truly means is the ability of a leader to be present in the moment… Here. Now.

In the context of this chapter, I'm thinking of leadership as our ability to influence or inspire other people. So, if leading means influencing and inspiring, we all need to lead in some contexts, even if we don't have the word in our job title.

The presence I'm talking about has a vibrancy. It feels alive. It offers you the ability to slow down and appreciate the moment. It helps you to connect and to access your own intuition. And it helps you to really see and take in another person.

Author and speaker Olivia Fox Cabane identifies presence as one of the three constituent elements of charisma, the other two being power and warmth.[1] Feeling that someone is fully there with us, in the moment, allows for that sense of connection. In contrast, when you are with someone, but you can see they are distracted, the message that this is likely to convey is: 'you don't matter to me now'.

The dimension of connecting within, in the here and now, sends out the message that the other person does matter. Being fully present with someone allows us to listen, to hear what they are saying, and notice our own reactions to what we're hearing. It allows us to respond to what we hear, rather than what we think we're hearing, which can happen when our thoughts are elsewhere.

Connecting in this way helps us at work. If you're leading change, for example, and encounter resistance, then really being present and listening to people's concerns can help you to respond accurately and sensitively. To give another example, it can be a powerful skill for networking. I can still remember a conversation with a photographer that I met five years ago at an event. The reason she stood out was the quality of presence that she emanated. The ability to bring this calibre of presence to our interactions will help us to build relationships that enhance our career prospects as well as our lives.

Aspects of the present

In their book *The Time Paradox*, Philip Zimbardo and John Boyd explore the time perspectives of past, present, and future.[2] As part of their work, they identified three ways of living in the present, which they refer to as present-hedonistic, present-fatalistic, and the holistic present.

Present-hedonistic is a perspective of becoming immersed in and enjoying the immediate sensual pleasures of life: having fun, partying, enjoying the moment. This time perspective is common among young people. Hedonistic living has positive aspects and helps us to squeeze the juice out of some pleasurable life experiences. But living constantly in a hedonistic present, with no concern for the consequences, can lead to risky behaviour, long-term problems such as addictions, and drifting through life with no sense of direction or purpose.

The present-fatalistic time perspective is a day-to-day way of living, when you don't believe that you have any control over your life and future. Things happen to you. Your chances are pre-determined. You don't plan to improve your life because you don't believe it's possible. You don't dare to dream. This is not an empowering place to be and, unsurprisingly, research shows a strong correlation between this time perspective and negative outcomes such as poverty. The lack of a sense of control or agency can lead to feelings of stress and depression or hopelessness. With this perspective, people may feel ground down by circumstances, but unable to conceive of things changing for the better.

The holistic present

The holistic present, in contrast to the previous two, is an expanded present-oriented perspective, which encompasses past, present, and future. It is a state of feeling connected with yourself and beyond yourself. You're able to make choices and to access the past and future without getting lost in them.

For me this perspective is summed up in the beautiful words of William Blake.[3]

To see a World in a Grain of Sand

And a Heaven in a Wild Flower

Hold Infinity in the Palm of your Hand

And Eternity in an Hour.

In this state, there is a sense of time opening up. There is an awareness of what is happening around you – sights, sounds, and sensations. A quietening and clarity of mind, which makes it easier for you to access fresh thoughts and feelings, memories, and ideas.

There are many paths into this state, and different words for it. *Mindfulness* has become a common term to describe a state of relaxed awareness of the present moment, a state where you are making conscious choices moment to moment, rather than reacting unthinkingly to external stimuli.

When and where have you experienced this state of being?

Mindfulness

The concept of presence, of being in the 'now', is often a part of spiritual teachings, perhaps because it can give a sense of time-lessness, a sense of being suspended from everyday thoughts and concerns. And it's a way into a sense of connection to something bigger than ourselves.

But it's not just the preserve of spiritual teachings. Mindfulness is increasingly being taught in school and work settings. It is, at heart, the skill of being present. *Mindful* magazine offers this definition:

> Mindfulness is the basic human ability to be fully present, aware of where we are and what we're doing, and not overly reactive or overwhelmed by what's going on around us.[4]

There is a significant evidence base on the positive effects of mindfulness. These can include a reduction in stress, a greater ability to focus, better working memory, improved ability to learn, more flexibility in the way we respond emotionally to triggers, and greater satisfaction in relationships.[5]

Meditation

Meditation is traditionally associated with spiritual practices, although in recent years has been widely adopted in health-care and workplace situations. And for good reason, as there is extensive evidence demonstrating the benefits of meditation. These include reducing anxiety, lowering blood pressure, and improving levels of concentration and work performance.[6]

At its core, meditation is simply the process of focusing your attention on one aspect of your experience. And then returning your attention to this focus whenever it wanders.

Practices: Coming into state of mindful presence

There are many ways that you can bring yourself into a state of mindful presence.

In this section, I'd like to introduce you to some of my favourite practices. These are the exercises that I return to most often and that have helped me develop my ability to come back to the present quite quickly. I'm not going to pretend that I spend my life in a state of eternal presence. I'm very far from it. But I do know how to come back to the present when I need to. Given how un-present I used to be, I can testify that this is a learnable skill, and one that can greatly enrich your life and of course your sense of connection.

Meditation with attention on the breath

In meditation, you may choose to focus on your breathing; observing an aspect of your breath, such as the air coming into and out of your nostrils, or the gentle rise and fall of your chest. Choose one aspect of your breathing to focus on and gently observe this aspect.

As you do this, you'll notice your mind wandering; you'll start thinking about something else. This is normal.

I've often heard people say something along the lines of 'I'm not good at meditation; my mind wanders'. But this is what minds do.

The value from meditation comes with noticing when your attention has wandered (which it will). And then gently bringing it back to the focus of your attention, in this case the breath.

Being gentle is important. As soon as you start to criticize yourself, for example, you are once again caught up in your thinking rather than your chosen focus. Notice this, and gently return your focus to the breath. If you start to think that this is boring, notice and gently return your focus to the breath.

Setting a timer can be helpful in starting meditation. If this is new to you, five minutes is plenty to start with.

Be kind to yourself. If you find the process distressing, stop and try another practice. For most people, mindfulness meditation is helpful and relaxing, but occasionally it can bring up thoughts and feelings that you find difficult to be with. So never force yourself. And be aware that there are trauma-trained meditation and mindfulness teachers if you feel you need additional support and guidance in this area.[7]

Returning your attention to a word or mantra

Another version of meditation is to focus on silently repeating a mantra or affirmation. This is one word or short phrase that you silently repeat in your mind. If you'd like to try this, then you could choose a word such as *Peace*, or *Shanti* (which is the Sanskrit word for inner peace).

It can sometimes be helpful to choose a word in another language as it may trigger fewer associations for you, and therefore the word itself is less likely to prompt your mind into thoughts.

Again, the process is one of noticing when your mind wanders and gently bringing it back to the word.

Mindful activity

Any daily activity can be used to practise presence and mindfulness. One example is to use handwashing as an opportunity for focused awareness.[8]

In this example, allow yourself to notice:

> The feelings of the tap, the water temperature, the sensation of your hands smoothing the soap around against each other, the texture of the towel as you dry your hands.

> The sounds of the water, the friction of your hands, background noises that may drift in.

The colour of your hands, the soap, the basin. Take an observing perspective, and if you find yourself drifting into judgement ('my nails look scruffy; I hate my age spots'), then try to let these go and just return to noticing what you see from a neutral perspective.

You can use a similar approach in most everyday activities such as making a cup of tea, cleaning a surface, gardening, and so on. As mindful activity can be practised in everyday life, it has the benefit of not needing any extra time to fit in. It may be an easier route into mindfulness for some people than a seated, eyes-closed process. And it has the benefit of helping you practise mindfulness as an everyday state of being that you bring more and more into your daily life.

Mindfulness in nature

A lovely way to practise day-to-day mindfulness is by spending time in nature and really taking in what's around you, the sights, sounds, and smells of the natural world.

Even if you live in a city, there will be somewhere where you can connect with trees and plants. You might choose to head to a local park, beauty spot, community garden, riverside, or lakeside.

Take a walk and direct your attention to one aspect of your experience. You might choose to take in what you see: the colours and shapes. You might choose to tune in to sounds as they arise, such as birdsong, the crunch of leaves or gravel underfoot, snatches of conversation from other walkers, the sound of running water, the background hum of traffic (let's get real here!). Or you might tune in to the physical sensations such as the feel of the ground under your feet, the temperature, and pressure of the air on your skin.

Whatever sense you choose to connect with, your aim is to notice rather than to think about what you are experiencing. Of course, you will find yourself thinking, but when you notice this is happening, gently bring your attention back to the noticing.

To give you an example, you notice that the leaves on the trees are starting to turn red and gold. This may trigger thoughts about autumn, the approach of winter, and so on. When you notice that your mind has drifted from the immediate visual information, bring it back. What do you see now?

I've noticed that focusing on the visual element is most likely to get my mind thinking, whereas focusing on physical sensation or on sounds makes it easier to stay in the present. What do you notice when you shift your attention? Is there one of your senses that tends to draw you more deeply into the present?

Movement and physical sensation

Dance or other forms of movement, such as martial arts, can help develop presence. For me, the body offers one of the easiest ways to come into the present holistic state. We'll explore this in more depth in the next chapter. In the meantime, when you find yourself drifting into the past or future, try bringing your attention back to an aspect of your body in the present. For example, feel into the soles of your feet on the floor, or feel into your fingers, wiggle them, and feel the inner sensations as you do this.

Recognize spontaneous moments

We encounter moments of intense presence from time to time without seeking them out. For me, looking into a baby's eyes can provide that moment of timelessness.

It can be that moment when we catch sight of a beautiful view or stunning tree or flower in bloom.

When that happens, take a moment to look and connect with the feeling it engenders.

You can't hold on to these individual moments for long, nor should you; you might miss what is to come. But you can notice those spontaneous occasions when your attention is brought into the present and, as far as possible, stay with that sense of being present as each moment transitions into the next.

Here and now

This is a beautiful exercise I learnt from Ram Dass's extraordinary book, *Be Here Now*.[9]

As you go through your day, occasionally ask yourself the question:

'Where am I?'

The answer is always 'Here'. Really feel that answer, the fact that you're 'Here'.

Now ask yourself:

'What time is it?'

The answer is always 'Now'. Really feel that answer; the present moment is 'Now'.

Summary: Crafting presence

- The ability to connect deeply with the present moment allows you to connect with yourself and therefore with others.
- Being grounded in the present gives you a perspective from which you can learn from the past and plan for the future.
- Simple mindfulness practices can help you gently return your attention to the present moment.

Your perspective?

How easy do you find it to stay present with your own experience and with other people?

To what extent do you tend towards living in the past or the future?

How do your preferred time perspectives affect how you show up at work?

What helps you to come into a state of presence?

Being aware of the present moment gives you a solid vantage point from which to deepen your connection with yourself. It can help you to stay both calm and alert in dealing with situations that you face in your day-to-day life and at work. And being grounded in the present allows you to make purposeful choices about where to direct your attention.

We'll now move on to explore more about how the awareness of physical sensation can help with developing this connected presence.

Chapter 2

Body whispering
Tuning in to the subtle
signals of body wisdom

Connecting deeply with ourselves requires us to connect with our whole being. This includes becoming aware of our bodies, our emotions, our values, and our thought processes.

In this chapter we'll focus on the value of connecting with our physical sensations and the link this has with our emotions. We'll explore ways to develop our awareness of our inner sensations, and how to tune in to them to help us manage our emotions, make wise decisions, and increase the warmth of our connection with ourselves and others.

The power of whole-body intelligence

Our bodies communicate with intelligence and wisdom, but tend to speak in whispers. They communicate through subtle sensations. If we ignore these subtle signals, our bodies may eventually start to shout or scream, to grab our attention through sensations such as physical and emotional pain.

Western cultures have tended to emphasize and prize the intellect. And many people have lost touch with a meaningful sense of being connected with their own bodies. The idea that the mind and body are separate is untrue. We may see our bodies as being in service of our minds, but in fact it's the other way around.

We are not minds suspended in flesh. Rather, our minds arise out of our physicality. Our brains are intimately connected to all the sensations in our bodies through the network of nerves. And thus, the mind arises from activity within both our brains and our bodies.

Given that our body and brain are one integrated system, increasing our connection with our body can open the door to an expanded, whole-body intelligence. We can change our minds through our bodies, for example with breathing exercises which affect our oxygen levels, and physical exercise which affects our hormone levels.

Your brain is extraordinary. It is an incredibly complex organ, containing 86 billion neurons (brain cells).[10] But the brain doesn't exist as a standalone neural powerhouse, kept alive by our body. It has evolved in service of one primary function, which is to keep us alive.

And your brain is not the only neural centre in your body. Research shows that our gut contains over 100 million neurons[11] and our heart contains at least 40 million.[12] This means there is intelligence within the body itself. The heart and gut neural networks may not think in words and pictures in the way our brains do, but they do communicate with our 'head brain' and play an important role in decision making.[13]

The first time I experienced a real felt sense of this connection was when I was in my twenties (a few years ago now!). I was quite a heavy smoker at the time. And in my attempt to give up the habit, I read Alan Carr's book *The Easy Way to Stop Smoking*. After so many years, I can't remember much from the book, apart from one enduring insight that it sparked for me. For the first time, I could clearly see a relationship between an embodied physical sensation and what was going on in my brain. I started to notice that when I wanted a cigarette, my brain started to imagine myself having a cigarette, predicting and creating a picture of me lighting up, and imagining how relaxing it would feel. But when I tuned in to my body's sensations, I noticed a sense of tension around my solar plexus. The signal started in my body and this seemed to trigger my thinking about smoking, which led to the unwanted behaviour. Knowing this, I found it easier to let go of my habit.

This insight contains the seed of a powerful tool that you can use to help yourself when communicating with others. If you ever feel anxious or worried about a social situation, try this. Gently take your attention off your thinking and away from all the stories you're telling yourself about the situation. And instead, bring your attention to noticing what's happening physically. What are the sensations in your body? Where are they located inside you? The better you get to know your body, the more easily you can connect to subtle sensations. And the more you practise asking yourself these questions, the more you'll be able to do this quickly and easily in different situations.

Once you've connected to the physical sensations, you might like to imagine that part of your body relaxing or releasing any tension. Recognize that there is a difference between the sensations and the story you're telling yourself which may be linked to the sensation. If you can focus on the physical sensations, and on adjusting them, this can affect your thinking. As an example, if you're breathing quickly and shallowly, then deliberately slowing and deepening your breathing can make a difference to your thinking. It works on a physiological level, affecting the chemistry of your endocrine system. And it also gives you something tangible and immediate to focus on, which in itself is likely to reduce anxious thoughts.

Embodied sensation

In thinking about your ability to sense your own body, be aware that there are three ways in which you can sense your physicality: exteroception, proprioception, and interoception.

Exteroception

This is the way in which your body senses the external world. It includes your sense of touch; your ability to sense the effects of pressure and temperature on your skin. Being aware of these sensations can help you feel connected to your immediate external environment.

Proprioception

This is your ability to sense where your body is in space. It is the sense that gives you balance. It can help you to sense and adjust your own posture. And it's the ability to sense the relative positions of parts of your body, for example allowing you to easily touch the tip of your nose with your finger.

Interoception

This is your ability to sense the interiority of your body, which allows you to bring your attention deeply into your joints, muscles, and connective tissue. Being aware of this allows you to feel deeply connected with yourself, to feel centred within your own physical being.

Connecting to inner sensation

Learning to connect with the (often subtle) sensations inside your body is a valuable skill. It will help you access information, for example areas of tension that may be early indicators of stress or unease with a situation at work. And you can develop this skill by bringing your attention into your body. If you're new to this type of practice, then it can help to do this in a quiet place and perhaps close your eyes to remove visual distractions.

As you get more skilled and experienced you can do this anywhere – as you're walking, dancing, preparing for a meeting. You can learn to keep a little piece of your attention on your interior landscape, even during connection with others or activities such as typing. I'm trying to do this as I type this paragraph: I'm aware of the words and aware of the feel of my feet connecting with the floor, and aware of the sensation of my fingers as I tap the keys.

The following exercise will help you to develop this skill.

Practice: Embodied connection

Find a comfortable place to sit, with your back straight and your feet on the floor.

You can also do this standing. In which case, take a comfortable stance with your feet on the floor (ideally without shoes if you can). Make sure your knees aren't locked.

The breath is a good place to start, as it's a place where the outside air meets your inside. So just take a moment and focus on your breathing. Don't try to change anything, just notice what's happening. What's moving inside your body?

Once you've really tuned in to what's happening now, you can start to make small adjustments. If you notice your breathing is short and laboured, then you can consciously extend the length of your inbreaths and outbreaths, and breathe more deeply from your abdomen. If you notice that you have tension in some part of your body, you can consciously choose to relax and release these areas.

Another version of the exercise is to do a body scan. You may choose to start with your scalp and face and then gently bring your attention down through your body. Allow your attention to travel to your shoulders, arms, hands. Then direct your attention through your torso, your back, and chest. Then down through your hips, thighs, knees, lower legs, ankles, and feet. Feel your feet being supported by the floor. Supporting you.

You'll find a recording guiding you through this practice in the *Connection Craft Kit* that accompanies this book. See page 212 for details.

If you experience discomfort

Tuning in to the interior of the body and developing an inner felt sense is, I believe, hugely valuable in connecting with ourselves. If you are new to this, please take it gently, and be aware that there is a possibility of discomfort, either physical or emotional.

If you are feeling physical pain in your body, you may not feel comfortable directing your attention to where the pain is. One approach can be to focus your awareness on other areas, rather than those that may be painful. Or, if you're able to, see if you can allow the sensations of pain into your awareness, but gently relax and soften around the sensations, consciously releasing any tension that might be making the pain worse.

On the emotional side, if you're not used to doing this and if you have become disconnected with your body, you might find that you experience some emotions. Emotions such as sadness or anger, maybe linked to trauma that happened in the past, can get locked into the body. For example, our fascia, which is the connective tissue found throughout our body, can hold tension. Sometimes the very fact that we're disconnected from our bodies is because on some level we are protecting ourselves from the risk of pain.

The role of movement in shifting emotions

Experiencing difficult or even unpleasant sensations and emotions isn't necessarily a bad thing, as long as you're not overwhelmed by them. The link between sensation in the body and the brain is very strong. Allowing yourself to feel and then deal with difficult emotions before they become overwhelming can be helpful. And a powerful way to help shift and transform emotion is through movement. But be aware that this can be contra-indicated if you have suffered from trauma; more on this later.

According to neuroanatomist Dr Jill Bolte Taylor, an emotion only lasts for 90 seconds as a physiological response.[14] The emotion is triggered, there is a chemical, physiological response, and then the chemical response dissipates. The reason why emotions appear to last longer is due to our thinking, which re-triggers our response and keeps us in the emotion.

I believe movement can be helpful in that it helps to shift your physiology, as well as giving you a positive focus for your mind. You don't need to analyse the emotion and risk getting caught up in your thinking, which can trigger further negative emotions. Instead, notice and acknowledge the feeling, and then use the feeling as a trigger for moving your body in a way that feels good.

So, if you feel some frustration, sadness, or anger, for example, then acknowledge this: 'I'm feeling angry', 'I'm feeling sad'. And then find a way of moving with this feeling, when circumstances allow. It may be going for a walk and allowing your anger to give you the energy to stride. It may be gently stretching, as if you're giving your sadness a little more space. It may be putting on some music and dancing. Allow yourself to literally move with the emotion, and focus on the movement rather than your thoughts about the emotion or feeling. Allow yourself to notice when your emotions change, whether this change is subtle or strong.

On sadness, if you feel tears arise, let them flow. I am grateful to a piece of wisdom from my mother. When I was upset, she would say: 'Have a good cry; it will make you feel better'. To this day, I'm quite easily moved to tears and let them flow, but after a few minutes I'm no longer holding on to the sadness.

And what if you find yourself overcome with strong emotions at work, for example, and don't feel it's appropriate to express them, given the situation, or the working culture or your role? There is a place for expressing emotion at work, in my view, as you show up more fully in the workplace, or when under-lying negative emotions may affect the way you do your job. But there are times when your responsibility as a leader, or a co-worker, or with customers means that you feel you may need to hold back. In this kind of situation, I suggest prioritizing giving yourself some space and time to move when you can. In the meantime, take a moment to acknowledge your feelings to yourself. You may also find it helpful to use an exercise such the one described below, focusing outwards.

If emotions are too strong or traumatic

If focusing inwards starts to feel overwhelming, it can be helpful to shift your attention away from the interior of your body and instead focus on the external physical world. A helpful technique can be to focus instead on what you see and hear: for example, name five red items in your environment, then notice and name four sounds that you can hear. This keeps you in the present and helps you not to get lost in your thoughts, but it reduces the intensity by keeping your attention focused outwards.

If you have experienced trauma in your life or encounter emotions that feel too strong to deal with, please seek professional support from an appropriately qualified therapist. With this advice, please don't shy away from going inside your body, so long as you are mindful of not going deeper than is right for you. There's always a need to take care of your body and emotional health, being aware of what is right for you at this point in your life.

The alternative to being comfortable with your inner sensation can be a sense of not being fully connected with yourself. It can even result in a kind of emotional numbness. In contrast, the sense of being fully connected with your inner senses brings many benefits. It can give you a sense of vitality, of feeling more alive. It helps you to be present with yourself and others.

When it comes to connecting with others, a sense of your own inner sensation can help you become more empathic. When you are tuned in to your inner sensations, you may find that you feel other people's sensations in your own body. This has positive aspects that are explored in Chapter 10. And if you're someone with a tendency to feel others' emotions too strongly, then movement can be helpful here too. You may for example choose to literally 'shake off' emotions. Start with one arm, standing up straight; just shake your arm as if shaking off what is unwanted. Then the other arm. Then, if safe, shake your individual legs, and even your torso, gently and to the extent that is safe for your body and state of health.

Accessing your intuition

Intuition is tuition (learning) from within. Using your intuition involves connecting with your inner knowing, your inner wisdom. Intuition will tell you what's right for you, which may be different to what's right for others. Intuition is also a way of accessing information for decision making that may be below your conscious awareness.

Intuition often comes from subtle sensations in the body. It's more of a whisper than a shout. We can hear our intuition most clearly when we slow down, get present, and tune in to a felt sense of what's right. Intuition doesn't make lists of pros and cons; it doesn't come from a logical linear thought process. It's a knowing.

Intuition is not a whim or a hunch. Sometimes we can think we're listening to intuition, but we're fooling ourselves. So, how do we tell the difference?

Can you think back to a time when you knew something was right (or wrong) for you, but you talked yourself out of that knowing?

A benefit of becoming more attuned to your inner body sensations is that it can help you access your intuition and intuitive decision making. By intuitive decision making, I mean making a decision using more than your conscious mind. Your conscious mind is still involved, but it's also open to information from within.

I see my intuition as a kind of inner mentor who communicates through subtle sensations in the body. You can journey to meet this inner mentor when you become quiet and still. Intuitive decision making is often felt as a subtle feeling. For me the sensation is a very subtle nudge that seems to start around my solar plexus and rises up. It's a tiny flutter, and it's very easy for me to ignore it or talk myself out of it. For example, I can think of instances where I've felt an inner nudge to perhaps send a message of support to somebody. But then I talk myself out of it, or get distracted: 'maybe I'll do it later'. And then the moment and the impetus is gone.

Part of getting better at using intuition is knowing what a wise impulse feels like for you. It's not necessarily the same as just doing something because you feel like it at the time. And intuition has its limitations. I believe it can be reliable when it's a decision that you make about yourself. It's about tapping into something that you feel deeply is right for you. And research shows that intuition can also be effective when you're making a decision in an arena where you have a lot of knowledge,[15] and where the subconscious processing power of your brain can draw on previous experience to predict what might happen next.

Intuition is not infallible, and if you're looking at a significant decision then it's wise to combine intuition and body wisdom with a rigorous intellectual approach to ensure you have a strong grasp of facts as well as feelings.

Practices

Sway Technique

The Sway Technique can help you to tap into wisdom within your body.[16]

Like all body-based techniques, you need to come back to a centred place to start with. So, start with taking up a comfortable neutral stance, back straight, knees relaxed. Take a few breaths until you feel relaxed and your mind is clear.

And then, from this centred place, ask yourself a question to which you know the answer is yes. For example, I might say 'is my name Felicity?' Ask the question clearly out loud, aiming to keep as relaxed as possible with your mind clear. Then just notice whether your body sways slightly in one direction or other, typically forward or back. Repeat this a couple of times with questions to which you're very confident of the answer, for example do you like a certain food or do you live in a specific place? See if you get a sway that seems clear and consistent for a yes.

And then shake this out; set yourself again into that relaxed centred stance. And ask yourself a question to which you know the answer is no. For example: 'Is my name [not my name]?'. 'Do I love eating [food you hate]?'. 'Would I like to do [an activity that you hate]?'. If I say: 'Would I love to go skydiving?', I get a clear no response! Notice which way, if any, your body sways when the answer is no. Is it different to when the answer is yes?

Like all techniques, it doesn't work for everyone, but you may find you get a clear and reliable sway in one direction or another. For me, I certainly get a very clear, slight, but distinct, sway which is consistently either forward or backwards, depending on my answers.

If you like the technique and it seems to be working for you, practise with statements to which you know the answer until you get really confident in the consistency of your body's response. You're not consciously trying to direct the sway; just stay upright yet relaxed, so that subconsciously your body will move you back and forth.

Once you're confident of this, you can use it to help you make decisions. To use in decision making, you need to ask a question to which the answer is a yes or no. For example: 'Should I take this course?'

Remember, it's not magic. It won't tell you anything about the outcome of a decision. But it can help you in situations where you feel stuck or going round in circles thinking about pros and cons, and would like to tap into another source of information.

Connecting with your heart

There is something very special about the heart. Connecting with your own physical heart area can transform how you feel about yourself and how you connect with others. The heart contains upwards of 40 million neurons and has its own form of intelligence. Consciously connecting with the area around your heart can help you connect more deeply with others.

A simple exercise is just to settle down with your feet on the floor and take a couple of slow gentle breaths. Then place your hand gently on your heart, maybe close your eyes if appropriate, and gently breath in and out for a few breaths. Imagine the breath is flowing in and out of your heart area. Allow your breathing to be slow and rhythmic. After a few minutes, open your eyes if they are closed, and notice how you feel.

I experience heart connection as very powerful. Where I'm facing a challenging encounter or simply going into a coaching conversation with someone, I find connecting with my heart for a few minutes can allow me to relax and connect with greater kindness and empathy.

The HeartMath Institute has undertaken extensive research into this area and has developed a number of evidence-based techniques to tap into the power of the heart.[17] I recommend their work if you'd like to explore this further.

Connecting within through movement

Movement is one of the most powerful state changers, mood enhancers, health preservers, and creativity stimulators available to us. And yet, for many people, it has been reduced to the rather dull concept of 'exercise'; seen as something that is good for us but not necessarily enjoyable.

In my view, movement should be enjoyable. If you haven't yet found a way of moving that you love to do, then keep looking and trying out different movement methods. It's like finding the right life partner. You may get on well with many people, but when you find the right partner, something clicks, and you know this is the person you want to spend your life with.

Movement by its very nature connects the body and brain. And research shows that different types of movement affect the brain in different ways.

A 2014 Stanford University study demonstrated that walking had a significant impact on creative thinking abilities compared to sitting.[18] Walking outside had the biggest impact. However, walking inside also increased levels of creativity.

My personal favourite way to move is to dance. Research into the effect of dance on mood indicates that dance has a positive effect on mood compared to other non-dance based aerobic activity such as cycling.[19]

Dance psychologist Peter Lovatt and cognitive psychologist Carine Lewis undertook a study which explored the impact of different types of dance on people's thinking. They discovered that dance which involved copying steps increased people's performance when it came to convergent thinking, for example solving a problem with a correct answer. And a more creative improvisational style of dance increased performance when it came to divergent thinking, such as coming up with different and creative uses for an everyday object such as a brick.[20]

Other movement systems which connect body and mind include Pilates, where you think into your body and make small, controlled movements which strengthen the muscles, particularly the intrinsic muscles, which are those close to the bones. Another is the Alexander Technique, which helps you develop a greater awareness of movement and posture, for a more balanced and aligned body. Both methods are often used to help people recover from injuries or pain related to joint or postural problems. But they also help develop mind-body awareness and can enrich our health and our lives.

Summary: Crafting body wisdom

- Connecting with your inner sensations gives you access to greater wisdom, self-knowledge, and intuition.
- Integrating the brain and body through movement and sensation helps you to move through, and process, emotions.
- Tuning in to the sensations of the body can give you a different perspective and integrates inner knowing with cognitive understanding.

Your perspective?

How easy do you find it to connect with your inner sensations?

What does an 'inner knowing' feel like for you?

What effects do different kinds of movement and exercise have on your body, mind, and mood?

How might connecting more deeply with your body affect the way you show up at work?

The power of connecting with the wisdom of your body and your physical sensations can put you more deeply in touch with your intuition. It can help you to make wise decisions and to manage your emotional state.

We'll now move on to think about how we can connect with our values. Greater awareness of our values can guide our choices at home and at work, and give our lives a deeper sense of meaning and purpose.

Chapter 3

Does this matter?
Values as your
trustworthy guide

Connecting with yourself involves getting to know, trust, and follow what is truly important for you. Your values can act as a guide in making decisions about how to behave and respond to situations. Integrating values in your life can help to give a sense of meaning and purpose to everyday activities.

In a culture where there is constant pressure for us to think and behave in certain ways, connecting with our values can help us make wise decisions and to behave in ways that feel authentic to us. It can help us decide which people and causes feel worthy of our time and attention. And it makes it easier to say 'no' when we need to.

Living to a clear set of values helps us to make decisions, at work and beyond. It can help us to build trust with other people because it's clear what we stand for. And we're more likely to be happier and successful at work when there is a good fit between what we care about and the purpose of the organization we work for.

This chapter offers ideas on how to identify and work with values to enrich all aspects of our lives.

The importance of living by our values

Australian nurse Bonnie Ware held many conversations with people at the end of their lives. When she asked people about any regrets they'd had in life, she noticed patterns in responses, which she then explored in a book: *Top Five Regrets of the Dying*.[21] The number one regret she found was: '*I wish I'd had the courage to live a life true to myself, not the life others expected of me*'.

One way you can connect more deeply with what is true to yourself is through a deliberate consideration of your values, and a conscious decision to live these values out in your life.

But how do we separate out what's true to ourselves from what others expect from us? We may know what our nearest and dearest want from us. And in fact, rebelling against parental expectations is part of growing up, so we sometimes choose to take a different path, at least for a while.

Yet there is also much that society expects of us that we might not consciously take into account. We are all subject to pressures from different people in our lives, from the cultural norms at our place of work, and the wider social culture.

Cultural expectations may be so embedded that we may not always be aware how they are directing our choices. External expectations may become internalized as assumptions and beliefs that we may not recognize or challenge when making decisions. To give an example, I was working with someone whose organization viewed competition between staff as the best way to boost performance. This person was taking this cultural norm for granted, so they were struck by hearing the experience of someone in a different company, which valued co-operation between staff and had a different reward structure, focused on rewarding team success rather than individual performance. For some people a competitive environment may feel exciting and motivating. But for many others, it feels pressurized and they thrive in a more collaborative culture.

A thoughtful exploration of values can help you connect with what you really care about in your life.

What are values?

Values are what really matters to you. That which you value.

Values are not goals. They are the *why* and *how* that underpin the behaviours and choices that you make in your life. Not the *what*.

The metaphor of a compass is sometimes used to represent our values. A compass can guide us in deciding in which direction we should head. It's not the map to a specific destination. Instead, it gives us a tool for navigating choice points.

For example, you might ask yourself: 'Should I prioritize the job with more money, or the job with social purpose?' This isn't necessarily a 'good' versus a 'bad' choice. It may be that you're at a point in your life where getting your finances on a stable footing, so that you can provide for family, is the guiding choice. Or it may be that your top priority is to align your values with that of the company you work for, even if it means less pay.

Our circumstances may mean that we can't always make choices that prioritize our highest values. But to live in a way that feels authentic, it is important to consider our values when making decisions and decide where we can compromise, and where the price is just too high.

Values can help you choose goals and directions that are true to you. And they also represent qualities you can integrate into your life now. To give you an example, imagine that generosity is an important value for you, yet money is tight, and you don't feel able to give in a financial sense. You can honour this value in other ways, such as giving time through volunteering, or giving genuine compliments and encouragement to others.

It is often possible to summarize values with single words. When identifying values, it's important to really dig down into what those words mean to you. For example, many people put family high on their list of values. But the way individuals interpret that word will be different. For one person, valuing family may mean being a provider. It may be a motivator for working hard and bringing in an income. For another person, family may be about working less and, instead, spending more time with the family. So, the same word will not mean the same thing to everyone, and it's important to choose words that are meaningful to you.

Discovering your values

Personal reflection

There are various ways that you can identify your values. And if you've never done a values exercise before, I encourage you to do one. I run these types of exercises in leadership training and with career coaching clients and often hear afterwards that these explorations were very valuable in helping people to consider their priorities and make decisions.

One way is to simply sit down with a notebook and reflect in writing about what matters to you. It can be helpful to consider both what you care about, those values that attract you; these are sometimes called 'pull values'. They pull you towards a course of action.

In contrast, you can also consider circumstances that trigger a negative reaction, when your values are being violated. These are sometimes called 'push values' in that they highlight ways of behaving that you are repelled by, that are not aligned with what you care about. And from this understanding, you can start to identify your positive (pull) values.

Here are some questions to prompt reflection.

Pull values

- What's really important to you?
- What are the qualities you respect or admire in others?
- What do you want your life to be about?

Push values

- What makes you angry?
- What words or behaviours trigger a negative response in you?
- What values are being threatened?

Once you've come up with some ideas, dig under these to see what's going on. For example, if you admire people who take a stand for the disempowered, then this may point to values such as justice, or equality, or courage. If you're made angry by injustice, then it may be that justice, or fairness, or equality are strong values for you.

Life visualization

Another great exercise for uncovering values is to project yourself forward in time and see yourself at your 90th birthday party. Imagine that you are surrounded by people that you love. It doesn't matter whether or not they will still be alive when you're 90. And as this is an imaginative exercise, anyone significant in your life can be there.

As you enjoy your day, you're thinking about all the things you're happy about in your life's journey. What are they?

And guests are coming up to you and telling you things that they've really appreciated about you. What would you really love to hear?

When you look back at life from that perspective, what are you proud about in the way you've lived your life? Your personal qualities? The choices you've made? The values that have guided your decisions?

Then come back to the present. Which of these values are you living in your life today? And which could you be living more deeply? Which values could you bring to the forefront of your decision making, day to day?

Listing values exercise

Another way of identifying values is to use a list of words as a prompt. When you use a word list, you may find at the start that you identify a lot of the words that resonate. It's then helpful to narrow down the list to those values that are most alive and important for you. It's not that the other values don't matter in your life. But if you're going to work with values for decision making, it's easier if you have a few guideline values that are most important for you at this point in your life.

There's a short list here, to get you started, and there's a longer list in the accompanying *Connection Craft Kit* that you can download if you'd like to (see page 212). This is a two-stage exercise:

Step 1: Go through the list below and mark each value as:

V: Very important to me

Q: Quite important to me

N: Not particularly important to me

Value	V/Q/N	Value	V/Q/N
Achievement		Hope	
Adventure		Humour	
Autonomy		Independence	
Beauty		Innovation	
Challenge		Integrity	
Communication		Intelligence	
Compassion		Love	
Competence		Loyalty	
Competition		Open-mindedness	
Courage		Order	
Creativity		Patience	
Curiosity		Power	
Dependability		Productivity	
Discipline		Prosperity	
Diversity		Recognition	
Effectiveness		Respect	
Empathy		Responsibility	
Equality		Risk taking	
Family		Safety	
Flexibility		Service	
Freedom		Simplicity	
Friendship		Spirituality	
Generosity		Strength	
Growth		Teamwork	
Harmony		Trust	
Health		Truth	
Honesty		Wisdom	

Step 2: Define your top five values

Go back through the list, review all your Very Important values, and select the five that are most important to you, at this stage of your life. Reflect on what each value means to you, and how you might live this value out in your day-to-day life and work.

Step 3: Reflect on compromises

Are there any important values that feel as if they are being continually compromised in your life? For example, you may value family, but be in a job that involves long or unsocial hours. These compromises are often a cause of stress. Are there changes that you can make in the short, medium, or longer term that will make it easier to live out this value?

What if values clash?

When you start thinking about your values, it's not uncommon to identify some potential areas of conflict between them. For example, you might value freedom. And you might also value security and see this as potentially in conflict with freedom. If this happens, have a deeper dig down into what you mean by these values.

As an example, when I was young, freedom was a high value for me. And having a secure home also felt important. My desire for security led me to buying my first flat as soon as I could. After moving into that flat, despite the mortgage, I paradoxically felt a greater sense of freedom than previously. Maybe it was because I now felt more secure so was able to give more attention to meeting my value of freedom. In my case, freedom was more about feeling free to make my own choices (rather than, say, the freedom to take off and travel around the world on a whim!).

If you become aware of a conflict, you could ask yourself whether there are ways to honour both values. For example, if financial prosperity and social justice are important to you, can you bring both values into play? An example is illustrated in the image below. One option could be to take a job that pays well and then donate intentionally to causes that support social justice. Another option could be a career in a sector with the potential for well-paid work which also has a social impact, such as some parts of the legal profession.

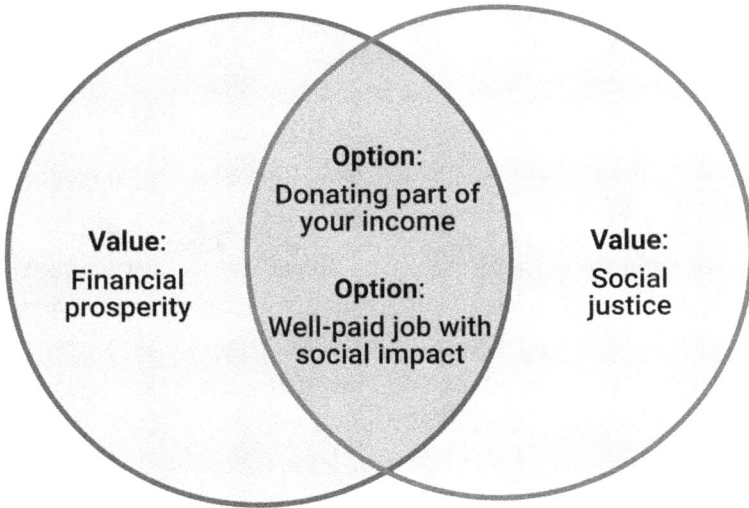

Bringing an understanding of your values into your life will help you feel more connected with what really matters to you. You can use this understanding to guide your choices. And when you notice a clash between two values, you are then in a better position to take a step back, observe what's happening, and use this expanded knowledge in making decisions.

Living by your values

Once you've identified your values, you can use them as a guide to how you want to show up in family, social, or workplace situations.

Values aren't goals. I've said this before, so let me expand this statement with an example. Say that you realize justice is a core value for you. This doesn't necessarily mean you need to change career. Yes, one option for people with this high value may be to qualify as a lawyer, and perhaps become a legal aid solicitor. But another way to honour this value is by allowing it to permeate everything you do in your family or at work. You'll want to make sure that people are heard and people are treated fairly. It may affect your spending choices. It may affect the decisions you make about where to donate your time and money for good causes.

Another example: say that kindness is an important value. You can be kind in all sorts of everyday interactions, with yourself and others. If you're in a situation where you could say something blunt or something a little bit mean or sarcastic, you can choose to be kind instead. Kindness doesn't necessarily mean you avoid difficult conversations, but it means you think carefully about how to approach those conversations in a way that both honours what you think and feel, and respects the other person's dignity.

One of my highest values is learning. One of the reasons I chose to work for myself back in 2003 was the sense that I wanted to create my own career by choosing subjects that I wanted to learn more about, and to build my skills in facilitating learning for others. I'm very happy with the choices I made to infuse my career with the value of learning. And when I met my husband, I was attracted by the fact that he's equally motivated by learning. This shared value has helped to underpin our life together.

So, values are not goals. But they provide a way of deciding which goals to pursue; where to focus your time and energy, and which goals to leave to one side. If health is a value to you for example, this can guide your decisions. But there's no one way to be healthy. You might decide to run marathons, eliminate sugar and alcohol, and eat a diet which ticks every health box. Or you might just use this value as a gentle choice to say no to that second glass of wine, and to make sure you go for a walk every day. So, the way in which that value shows up in life will be different for different people. But it will guide your choices so that you ultimately prefer to choose the healthy option rather than an option that will not be so good for your body or mind.

Practices: Bring your values to life

Try consciously working with your values, using them as guides to direct your life choices, day to day. Allowing values to permeate your life can be motivating and give everyday life a sense of meaning. Here are three suggestions for how to do this.

1. You could start your day by thinking of one value that you want to focus on and play with ways to bring this into the way you connect with people.
2. You could spend five minutes writing about one of your values in your journal. What does this mean for you? How do you already live out this value in your life? How could you live out this value to a greater extent?
3. You could draw a compass with your top four or eight values in the main directions, and refer to this when you have a decision to make, as part of your decision-making toolkit.

Mismatched values at work

Connecting with your deepest values may bring up real-izations that in some part of your life, there is a mismatch between who you are and who you want to be, against what is expected from you.

This is probably most often experienced at work, where you may realize your values are not well aligned with those of your company. I remember many years ago working for an orga-nization in which there was very little sense of teamwork. There were no team meetings or opportunities to connect with others. This contrasted with my next job, which was a year-long contract. Although only a contractor, I felt very much part of the team. The department included me in meetings, and offered opportunities for learning and taking on new responsi-bilities within the role.

The values of an organization are not always apparent. I remember being interviewed for the job in the first example and hearing plenty about being part of the team. But nothing in practice bore this out. Former MIT management professor Edgar Schein has differentiated between what he calls espoused values – these are the kind of values you'll find on a company website – and the deeper underlying assumptions, which are the cultural norms of behaviour within an organization, often followed unconsciously by those who have absorbed them.[22]

A mismatch of values doesn't mean the organizational values are wrong in themselves, just that they aren't a good fit for you, whilst also recognizing that some organizations seem to alienate more good staff than others. There is research evidence to back up the value of positive organizational behaviours and culture. Discussing organizational culture in detail is beyond the scope of this book, but the type of communication skills described in the *connecting with* section of this book will have a positive impact at work.[23]

Becoming aware of a serious mismatch of values can trigger a career change, either to an organization that's a better fit for you or even a completely new field of work, or self-employment. But realistically, a change of job is not always going to be an option, at least in the short term. If you find yourself in the position of being uncomfortable with the values of your organization, what can you do?

Commit to being as true to yourself as you reasonably can to work. If collaboration is a value for example, you can look to see if there are some opportunities to work more collectively, even if the overall culture of the organization is quite competitive. Values are about how you do things, and there will always be aspects that are within your control. You can also set out to use whatever influence that you do have at work to good effect. If you're a leader or manager, there may be actions you can take in the way you lead your team that will have a positive impact.

And look for ways to live out your values in other aspects of your life. It may not be comfortable or sustainable to feel compromised at work. But if this is necessary in the short term, then finding a balance elsewhere can allow you to maintain that connection with what matters to you.

Summary: Crafting values

- Identify your values by connecting consciously to what's important for you. And pay attention to subtle sensations that may indicate you're not making choices in line with your values.
- Notice where there are potential conflicts between different values and see if you can find ways to

acknowledge and honour values that aren't currently being reflected in how you're living your life.

- Integrate values into your thinking and behaviour choices to infuse everyday life with a greater sense of purpose. Deliberately choose to act in line with your values, in the way you connect to both yourself and others.

Your perspective?

What do you value? What matters to you?

How do you know that your choices are aligned with your values?

How do you feel when you don't act in alignment with your values?

Are there changes you need to make to live more fully in line with your values?

In this chapter you've explored ways to connect with what's most important to you by taking time to consider your values, along with ways to deliberately bring them into how you show up in life and at work.

Now we'll go on to look at how we can better understand our cognitive thought processes. We'll consider ways to use our minds even more effectively, with ever-increasing self-awareness. Understanding how we think allows us to relate effectively to other people in a way that's both true to ourselves and respects difference.

Chapter 4

Getting out of your own way Uncovering clarity by noticing your own thought processes

Connecting with yourself includes developing an ability to understand *how* you think. Not just *what* you think, which can vary from minute to minute. Your thoughts can shape the way you see the world and the way you behave. But you don't have to define yourself by your thoughts. As Buddhists say: '*you are not your thoughts*'.

If you can truly see that people are not their thoughts, then how much easier might it be to treat yourself with kindness rather than self-judgement? How much easier might it be to connect with those who may think very differently? How much easier might it be to approach conversations with curiosity, compassion, and an open mind?

In this chapter, we'll look at some powerful concepts to help you notice your own thinking patterns and work with them in a positive way:

- fusion and defusion;
- the observing self;
- inner critic;
- acceptance.

Fused with your thoughts

A helpful metaphor for understanding how our thoughts affect us is that of fusion. When two pieces of metal, or bones, fuse together, they are joined tightly as one. Similarly, when our identity is fused with our thought patterns, our current thoughts and emotions make up our lived experience in that moment. So, when we are fused with angry thoughts and feelings, we 'are' angry.

But if we can take a metaphorical step back and notice our thoughts and feelings, including noticing physical sensations in our body, then we are no longer 'fused' with those thoughts and feelings. This process is known as *defusion*.[24]

A valuable learning for me has been the ability to differentiate between who I am and how I think. I can think angry thoughts without being an 'angry person'. And once again, connecting with the present moment allows us to take a metaphorical step back, to observe our thoughts, to get to know our thoughts, and to understand that our thoughts are not 'reality'.

The observing self

The perspective from which we can notice our thoughts is sometimes called *the observing self*. And as soon as we're able to notice our thoughts or feelings, we have in that moment an opportunity to connect with the part of us that observes. We have more than one perspective on our state of mind. And if we can connect with the observer, we can choose to make a behavioural choice from that perspective.

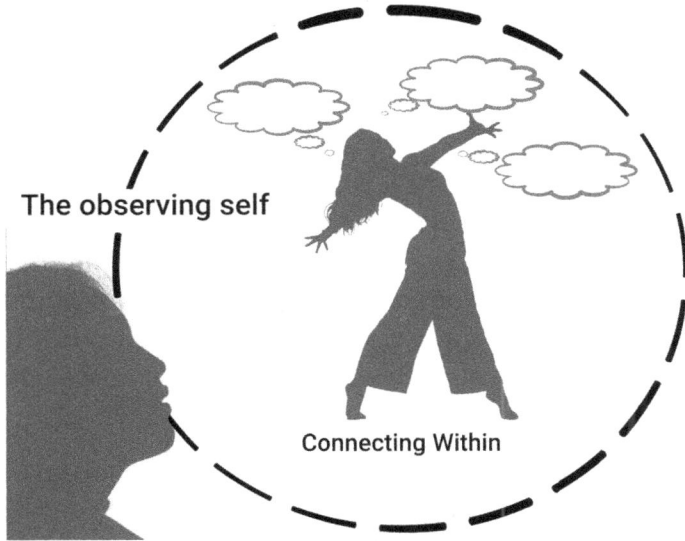

The observing self

Connecting Within

For example, you may notice that you're having angry thoughts towards someone: 'they've let me down', 'they lied to me', 'how could they...?' You may be feeling sensations such as a raised heart rate, racing thoughts, or tension in your muscles.

Rather than reacting and speaking some of these thoughts out loud, which you might do when anger is all consuming, connecting with the observing part of yourself offers you more choices.

For example, you might decide not to speak, but instead to focus your attention on connecting with the sensation of your feet on the floor or slowing down your breathing. If and when circumstances permit, you might go for a walk or a swim, or put on some music and allow the energy of anger to flow through you in movement or dance.

This doesn't mean that it's never right to express anger. But I know from my own repeated experience that speaking in the heat of the moment can lead to regret. I've spent a lot of time in my life apologizing for losing my temper. Learning how to take a step back and deciding how best to express myself has helped me to gradually learn ways to communicate with the benefit of perspective, rather than being hostage to a reactive response.

Defusion is *not* disassociation. The latter is a state of numbness or disconnection, often accompanied by a sense of feeling detached from our body – this is definitely not the message of this book. Disassociation can be a coping strategy or an indication of extreme stress or some mental health condition.[25] It can be an extreme version of the 'freeze' stress response and may need specialist support.

In contrast, in defusing, we recognize that we are the ones experiencing the thoughts and feelings; they are not separate from us, but nor are they our whole reality. As soon as we're able to notice that we are experiencing thoughts and feelings, there is some separation. We can identify with the 'I' that notices our thoughts and feelings. And this gives us enough distance to make a choice.

Your inner critic

The inner critic is a common term for that negative and nagging inner voice that most of us experience at times. If you've ever 'beaten yourself up' for some perceived inadequacy or stupidity, this is the inner critic.

I know this one well, especially in the past. Running training courses, for example, means that you are 'on show' much of the time. I would come back from an overall successful course or talk and go over and over one small error or aspect that I wasn't happy with: 'Why did I say that!'. Often no one else seemed to have even noticed my perceived mistakes.

Learning how to defuse, to notice the inner critic, and to identify with the 'I' that is noticing has been transformational
for me. And these days, even though I sometimes lapse into
self-criticism, I find that once I notice that I'm doing it, I can
more easily choose to let that thinking go. It certainly makes
me much more relaxed as a trainer and speaker.

Developing the observer perspective

It's important to say that defusion is about noticing what's
happening. It's not about trying to drown out your inner critic
by arguing with this part of yourself, or by trying to drown
out this voice with positive phrases (sometimes known as affirmations). Techniques such as affirmations can be valuable and
worth trying. However, my personal experience is that defusion can be gentler and more effective.

Defusion is a practice of noticing and acknowledging your
thoughts and feelings. It's about not over-identifying with that
voice, instead seeing it as a manifestation of your thinking in
that moment. Once you've noticed this critical voice, you can
then make a choice. Maybe the inner critic has a point that you
can learn from, in the way of constructive feedback. Maybe it
is just comparing you with some imaginary 'perfect you' that is
unlikely to ever exist.

The 'I' that can notice exists in the present. As discussed in
Chapter 1, being able to connect with the present moment
allows you that flexibility to make choices, not only choices
about what to do, but about what to pay attention to: the critical voice or the part of you that can observe the voice. This
observing self, this 'I', is the perspective from which we can
make wiser choices.

How do you know you're connecting and identifying with the observing self? Generally, you will feel a sense of calm. You're much more likely to be grounded in the present moment; aware of your body, aware of sensations, and aware of your thought processes.

My experience is that when I'm emotionally fired up, I find myself slipping between fusion and defusion. I may be angry because of something that's been said and feel myself completely taken over by those thoughts and feelings. Then I remember to defuse, I connect with my body sensations, I notice my thoughts, and am able to objectively observe my inner dialogue. And a couple of minutes later, I'm lost back in that angry thinking. The process of defusion does take practice.

Practising it on everyday frustrations is helpful, so that when you're really faced with a difficult situation, it's easier to take that step back and observe yourself (and others) with more gentleness and perspective.

Practices

Notice and name

Notice and name the thoughts and feelings that you are experiencing from the perspective of the part of you that is a neutral observer.

It can be helpful to first name the thought or feeling or sensation. Consciously naming our thoughts and feelings helps to give us some distance. It allows us to start seeing them from an observing perspective.

For example:

> 'I'm thinking that I always mess up.'
>
> 'I'm feeling sad.'
>
> 'I'm feeling a tension in my stomach, a tightness in my solar plexus.'

Then acknowledge that you are noticing that you're experiencing the thought or feeling. By noticing that we're noticing, we take the defusion process a step further.

For example:

> 'I notice that I'm thinking that I always mess up.'
>
> 'I notice that I'm experiencing a feeling of sadness.'
>
> 'I notice that I'm aware of a feeling of tension in my stomach.'

The purpose of this exercise is to help you identify with the observer, the 'I' who can notice these things, and is as much a part of you as the critical thoughts or uncomfortable emotions or sensations. As an example, it's possible to feel sad and to notice that you're feeling sad, without needing to disassociate from the emotion and pretend it isn't happening.

Over to you

Practise using the following words; bring in your own thoughts and feelings where indicated by xx.

> 'I'm having xx thought.'
>
> 'I'm feeling xx.'
>
> 'I'm thinking xx.'

'I notice that I'm having xx thought.'

'I notice I'm thinking xx.'

'I notice that I'm feeling xx.'

'I notice xx sensation in my body.'

It's worth practising doing this regularly during day-to-day life or in response to small irritations, so that it's more likely that you'll be able to do it then when triggered.

Notice that I'm thinking

Another approach involves simply noticing that you have some thoughts or thinking going on. For example, you may notice that your mind is racing with things that could go wrong, maybe at an interview, or a presentation, or a conversation. Rather than naming the individual thoughts, you could try simply noticing that you have some unhelpful 'thinking' or 'thoughts' going through your mind. This approach is sometimes easier than naming the content of thoughts as so often thoughts can lead off into trains of new thinking before we realize that it is happening. This noticing technique acknowledges that we have some thinking going on, without necessarily having to engage with the content of our thoughts.

Do this with gentleness. Your mind is trying to help keep you safe with these thoughts, but it's not necessarily helpful to engage with them. You could try saying 'thanks mind' or 'ok mind' to acknowledge that your mind is trying to help you, rather than metaphorically fight with fearful or unhelpful thinking.

Mindfulness practices

This ability to take the perspective of an observer can be developed by present-moment and mindfulness practices, discussed in Chapters 1 and 2, as well as the notice and name technique described above.

This isn't always easy. Even having practised this approach for some time, I notice that I still slip back and forth between perspectives. I'm angry and feel like lashing out verbally, then connect with the observing self and take a few breaths. But if the triggers continue, I might notice I'm back in angry thoughts again, and repeat the process. Like any skill, this gets easier and more intuitive with practice.

Snow globe visualization

A metaphor that can be helpful is that of a snow globe. When we shake the globe, the swirling flakes are like our thoughts and feelings that swirl around our psyches. The snowflakes can be beautiful and give us a rich experience. But they can also obscure our view of what's really going on and distort our perspective. Coming back to the present, and taking a gentle observer position, can help the flakes to settle.

If you're feeling overwhelmed with racing thoughts and feelings, try settling down and imagining that you are in a snow globe and surrounded by those swirling thoughts. Imagine that you are just sitting there, watching the flakes whirl around, and knowing that if you sit quietly and just watch them, they will gradually settle and you will start to see a beautiful landscape around you.

Accepting what is

A related and helpful concept is that of acceptance. By acceptance, I don't mean a kind of passive resignation to unsatisfactory circumstances. It's not taking the present-fatalistic perspective, as described in Chapter 1. It's not about passively giving up hope, nor neglecting to make behavioural or circumstantial changes if they're needed.

Instead, it's about accepting that thoughts, feelings, and circumstances are as they are. It's about accepting our external and internal realities, rather than fighting them. By allowing acceptance, it can paradoxically make it easier to make changes. It frees up our attention and energy to focus on finding solutions and developing our aspirations. Psychologist Carl Jung has stated that: 'We cannot change anything until we accept it. Condemnation does not liberate, it oppresses'.[26] Learning to accept what is, without judgement, opens the door to more choices.

A technique I find helpful here is one I call 'Yes... And...' To give you an example, imagine you'd just been turned down after a job interview, and this has triggered some negative thinking about everything you did wrong or, worse still, what's wrong with you. Now imagine instead that you have used defusion skills if needed to step back from racing thoughts to notice and name them. Then, whilst acknowledging what has happened, use the word 'and' to expand your awareness so you can see the situation in a wider perspective.

> Yes, I accept that I didn't get the job; yes, I could have prepared better for some questions; yes, I feel disappointed; yes, I feel anxious about when the next opportunity will come up...

> *And* I achieved an invitation to an interview; *and* I have the support of my family; *and* the sun is shining today – I could go for a walk; *and* I have my health...

Acceptance is about facing up to, and acknowledging, disappointment and other negative thoughts and feelings, whilst also acknowledging that they are not the only data point in the multi-dimensional reality in which you live. This is the reason why it's important to use the word 'and' in this practice, rather than 'but'. It's about including and gently making space for all your thoughts and emotions, both negative and positive. It's not about trying to force yourself to only 'look on the bright side'.

There is certainly a time for reflecting on something like an unsuccessful interview to learn from the experience and consider ways to improve if needed. But a good time to do this might be after you've come to terms with the initial thoughts and feelings and gained that sense of acceptance, not when you're in the midst of negative emotions.

Practice: Opening up

Practise using the 'Yes... And...' technique on some aspect of your life that isn't going as well as you'd like it to. The approach acknowledges what is and puts it in a wider context. Here are some examples:

> Yes, I'm disappointed to have missed out on that promotion... And I'm aware that my colleagues in my current role appreciate me... And staying where I am for now will give me more time and energy to consider studying for a higher qualification...

> Yes, I'm angry at having been ripped off... And I'm fortunate to have found support in dealing with the situation... And I have learnt something valuable...

> Yes, I'm frustrated at not being able to leave the house.... And I'm grateful to have some work to do at home... And I'm grateful for a comfortable house... And this will give me more time for cooking and reading...

Summary: Crafting clarity

- Notice sensations, thoughts, and feelings from the perspective of the observing self: 'I notice I'm having the thought that…'
- Accept difficult situations by acknowledging them, but putting them into a wider context, integrating a whole range of thoughts or feelings without allowing them to colour your whole view on the world.
- Make decisions on how to communicate based on these wider and calmer perspectives.

Your perspective?

What are the common/habitual thought patterns that you notice in yourself?

How do you deal with disappointments in your life or career?

What difference could it make at work if you were able to take more of an observer perspective when dealing with difficult situations?

How easy do you find it to expand your awareness, so that it encompasses both positive and more difficult thoughts and feelings?

In this chapter you've considered ways to connect with the observer part of yourself and how this can help you to respond more effectively to circumstances. And how accepting thoughts and emotions whilst expanding your awareness can offer you a wider perspective on a situation, without having to deny or suppress difficult thoughts and feelings.

We'll now go on to look at other aspects of our thinking, exploring the stories we tell ourselves and the metaphors we use. Connecting with our myriad stories and metaphors can help us to understand ourselves better and open doors to new ways of understanding other people.

Chapter 5

Your inner landscape
Exploring metaphor
and story as a way of
understanding and changing
your experience of the world

As human animals, our brains and bodies are the product of billions of years of evolution. All human beings share common ancestors, and we are one species. We are the same, and yet are also each utterly unique in the way we experience the world.

The complexity of our brains means it is inevitable that we all see the world in subtly different ways. As Lisa Feldman Barrett puts it, 'All humans share a single, basic brain plan with about 120bn neurons and two hemispheres, right and left. But the neurons inside every skull wire themselves differently'.[27]

Although there are as many ways of seeing the world as there are people, there are common themes that emerge again and again within human cultures. These are linked to the physical ways in which we experience reality through the filters of our brains and bodies.

Consciously exploring our own experience of the world can help us understand ourselves better. And when we come to connecting with others, it is important to maintain a sense of interest and curiosity in their experience of their world. How does it differ from ours?

In this chapter, we'll look at the role that metaphor plays in the way we construct our experience, and at the way narrative and story is used to link and make sense of events in our lives.

The role of metaphor in understanding our experience

The word metaphor originates from the Greek word *metaphora* meaning 'to transfer'. Metaphors are often thought of as a literary device, but in reality the metaphors we use are more than that and are far more powerful than we may have realized. They can shape the way we experience the world at a deep level.

In *Metaphors We Live By*, authors George Lakoff and Mark Johnson explore how we structure our experience metaphorically. Metaphor is a way of describing something by likening it to something different. A theoretical concept may be experienced in terms of something concrete that exists in the physical world. Metaphor allows us to link the qualities of unrelated ideas, which may open up new thinking or different ways of seeing.[28]

For example, we can consider ideas as food: 'that gave me food for thought', or as plants: 'I'm nurturing the seed of an idea', or as money: 'this idea enriched my life'. Time can be experienced in many metaphorical ways, including as a substance (time slipped away), or as money (spending time).

Lakoff and Johnson argue that metaphorical understanding is much more than just linguistics. Metaphors come from the fundamental structure of our experience, and the reason so much of our language is metaphorical is because it reflects this innate structure.

For example, we tend to describe positive emotional stages as being higher (his mood lifted; her spirits rose), and more negative ones as lower (this brought me down; I'm feeling low). Lakoff and Johnson suggest there may be a physical basis for these correlations. When we're happy and confident we have a more upright posture, and when we're depressed we tend to have a more slumped posture or want to lie down.

Another example is the link between physical and emotional warmth or coldness. We may say that we warmed to someone straight away, or that we feel comfortable in a certain situation. Contrast that with the idea of feeling chilled to the bone by a horrific murder or being at the receiving end of someone's icy stare. As babies we are completely dependent on our caregivers, and if we are not kept warm, we will die, so the link between warmth and safety is hardwired early on in our lives.

Deep metaphors structure how we see the world. For example, we may refer to having a close connection with a friend or sibling even if they live in another country. The sense of physical closeness is metaphorically transferred over into our sense of the nature of the relationship. If we then start to dig more deeply into that sense of closeness, we might feel our connection as an invisible cord that links us across the miles, or a sense that part of them is a precious jewel centred in our heart and always accessible. Without exploration, we might not be aware of some of these metaphors. And the very concept of exploration can be seen as a metaphor for discovering more about the landscape of our experience. We can burrow deeper or widen our field of discovery. We can leave parts of ourselves behind or take them with us on our journey.

Understanding the metaphors that we live by can help us understand ourselves and others more deeply. If we are willing to entertain our use of metaphor as much more than being a 'figure of speech' this can help us to understand how we are structuring our experience of the world. This understanding connects us with ourselves and enriches our experience of life. It can also spark our curiosity in other people's metaphorical experiences, which helps us appreciate them at a deeper level.

The role of metaphor in changing our experience

An exciting aspect of working with metaphor is that it offers the potential to change your experience of life. Once we recognize some of our deep metaphors, this opens the door to changing them. Changing our inner metaphors offers us the potential to make changes in our outer world, as it can enable us to see, interpret, and respond differently to the world around us.

Through training in a process known as symbolic modelling,[29] I've explored some of my own metaphorical representations, and have facilitated the exploratory process for other people. It's fascinating to experience and observe both common themes and always-present differences in how people construct their experience at a deep level. You can do this inner exploration on your own or with the support of a facilitator, trained to ask questions that will help you identify your own metaphors without imposing their own.

To give you an example, in my coaching and facilitation work, I may hear a client talk about facing a barrier, or an obstacle, or coming up against a brick wall. The person may even physically gesture to the space where the wall is. This communicates a sense in which this wall is representing something real in the way the person sees the world.

When this happens, once I have the other person's permission to work with their metaphors, my response might be to ask the following question:

'And when there's a brick wall, what would you like to have happen?'

This question acknowledges the reality of the wall within the other person's metaphorical landscape, and then invites the other person to think about what they would like to happen within the world of the metaphor.

I've heard responses along the lines of 'I'd like a door to open up…' or 'I'd like a ladder to climb over the wall…'. By metaphorically exploring the door, or the ladder, this line of questioning can open up new ways of thinking.

The way of exploring metaphor is powerful because your exploration comes directly out of your own inner metaphorical experience, rather than another person's interpretation of your experience. An example of the latter approach might be if a coach or facilitator asks you if there's a way that you can climb the wall. This question would come from the other person's idea of the wall, with an assumption that climbing is the way forward. This is more restrictive than an approach based on Clean Language questions, which enable you to explore your own wall, in your own way.

Exploring your metaphorical landscape

To explore further the concept of metaphor and changing metaphors, I'd like to draw on the overarching metaphor of an inner landscape. Here are a few examples of how people might describe their inner experience. How might these metaphors affect how you feel about a situation?

'I'm on a rocky road.'

'I can't see the wood for the trees.'

'I'm on the edge of a cliff.'

'We're in uncharted territory.'

The power in metaphor is coming up with something yourself that describes the way you're feeling. Once you've articulated a metaphor that truly reflects how you are feeling, you might like to work with this and see if you can shift your experience.

Working with changing metaphors should always be done within the positive context of an outcome that you want to have happen. Because metaphor is powerful, you want to be turning your attention towards your desired outcome, not towards something that you don't want.

The way to ensure you do this is by using a specific, outcome-focused, question. If you're asking yourself the question, the phrasing is:

'And when [unhelpful metaphor], what would I like to have happen?'

So, if we take the example of 'I can't see the wood for the trees', the question would be:

'And when I can't see the wood for the trees, what would I like to have happen?'

And you ideally answer the question in the context of the metaphor. For example, you might come up with:

> *'I'd like to take a helicopter and fly above the forest, to see where it leads...'*

> Or *'I'd like to settle down in a clearing, and wait to see if a path opens up for me...'*

> Or *'I'd like to push ahead in one direction, and see where it takes me...'*

Notice whether, and to what extent, your response to the metaphor moves your thinking forward, in the context of the real-world situation where 'you can't see the wood for the trees'.

Working with metaphor in this way is not an everyday approach for most of us; a good starting point is just to keep your radar open and notice when you and others are using metaphor. We use them all the time, so you won't be short of opportunities to notice them.

If this approach strongly appeals, you might even like to experience a session with a facilitator trained in Clean Language and symbolic modelling.[30]

Practice: Noticing metaphor

As you go through your day, take a minute or two here and there to observe and notice your own metaphors.

What metaphors can you pick out in your thought processes?

What metaphors do you use in conversation?

What do these metaphors say about the way you see the world?

The stories we tell: Weaving our own narratives

Storytelling has been used throughout human history in interpersonal communication, and we'll talk more in Chapter 9 about the role of storytelling in connecting with others.

We also tell stories to ourselves all the time. Every time we tell a story, even a true story about ourselves, we pick out certain facts and make them connect. We weave them into a narrative, which both helps us make sense of our history and influences the choices and paths we take to the future. Stories link cause and effect: 'This happened to me in the past and therefore this is how I am in the present'. We tell ourselves stories about what we can and can't do.

'I'd never have the confidence to speak in public.'

'I can learn to speak in public.'

'My family didn't share their emotions, and that's why I tend not to let people know how I'm feeling.'

'My family didn't share their emotions, so I've learnt how important it is to connect with my feelings and talk about them with others.'

'No, I don't have the experience for this project.'

'Yes, I can take on that project; I have most of the knowledge and skills and can fill in any gaps with relevant training. It will be exciting to work on something new.'

Our stories can empower or limit us. We construct our history by storytelling it into reality. In the words of Steve Jobs: '...you can't connect the dots looking forward; you can only connect them looking backward'.[31]

So yes, we all tell ourselves stories. But how often do we stop to think about why we choose to tell them the way we do? Do we think about how our inner narratives affect the way we see ourselves and the world around us?

Think about the stories you tell yourself. Stories about who you are, what you've done, how you got to where you are now. If I asked you 'What's your story?', how would you choose to reply? Do you recognize the extent to which you join together aspects of your past into a story, with explanations drawing on cause or effect, or serendipity, or destiny?

We tell ourselves stories about our past – how did we get here? We tell ourselves stories about our future. What will happen in our lives? What is possible for us? These stories shape and are shaped by our identity.

For example, the story of our family history can affect our sense of who we are. But our knowledge of our family history is always going to be partial, based on certain events or perspectives that were important to our ancestors. We can honour traumatic events in our family history, whilst also drawing lessons and narratives from it that are empowering. We can also acknowledge difficult stories from our personal or collective history, whilst looking for ways to transform the stories where we can. The ancient and symbolic myth of the phoenix rising from the ashes provides a metaphor for transformation and renewal, where that is needed. The fact that we are here means that our ancestors were successful in surviving the vicissitudes that have affected people throughout human history, and their strength is in us.

Heroes and villains in our own tales

In our own stories, we are the protagonist. We may be the hero, we may be the victim, but in either case we are the centre of the narrative.

In telling our own story, the tendency is to cast ourselves as the hero. We look out through our eyes; we see the world from our perspective. We bring other characters into the story such as an antagonist or foe. We narrate the difficulties that we've overcome and may acknowledge the helpers, the people who guided and supported us. But ultimately, we are the heroes in our own story, and it's the story of our transition into who we are now.

We may sometimes tell ourselves a story where we cast ourselves as the villain. This may happen if we're beating ourselves up for being mean or unkind or doing something we wish we hadn't done. But more often than not, we find a story that somehow justifies or excuses what we've done. We tell a story that provides an explanation for why, on this occasion, we behaved as we did. Thus we can maintain our sense of self as the 'good guy'.

But reality is much more complex than the neat structure of a story. Most people are not heroes or villains most of the time. Decent people can do selfish things; sensible people can do silly things; kind people can say something thoughtless.

Our lives are a patchwork of incidents, thoughts, feelings, reactions, and interactions. We need to weave them together to make sense of ourselves. Our stories help us to simplify reality, and to maintain a sense of continuity between the person we are now and our former selves. Storytelling helps us navigate and make sense of our lives and build our sense of self.

Our stories are necessarily partial and selective, and they can be changed. But we are also potentially lost without a story of who we are, what we were, and how we came to be. We look for patterns in our own behaviour and reaction and say: 'this is who I am'. We own some behaviours and separate ourselves from others. We re-invent ourselves, and re-source, and re-store ourselves.

We are not our stories

It's important to recognize that a story is not the truth; it is a perspective.

We are the storyteller not the story. Once we see this, it can help us to carry our stories more lightly. It can free us up to change. And when we recognize that our sense of who we are may be a construct of a certain familiar story, we may choose to set ourselves in an updated narrative.

If you recognize that you are telling yourself a disempowering story, you can rewrite it. See it differently; tell it from another perspective.

For example, most of us can find stories where we've made mistakes at work. And we can do this from the perspective of what we learned from the experience, and how this has built our character, or may help us in the future to grow into the person we want to be or find the career path that will allow us to thrive.

Realizing we are not our stories can offer a kind of liberation. As the storyteller, we can identify with the observing self, and bear witness to the ever-changing swirl of reality and interpretation around us.

Our future comes out of actions that we take now in the present. And our experience of the present is closely linked to the stories we tell of how we got here. By retelling our stories, we can potentially write ourselves a different future.

Practice: Retell your story

The purpose of this exercise is to practise telling some of your stories in a new way.

Tell a story of a pivotal moment in your life and the impact this had. You could do this exercise with a friend by sharing your stories out loud. Or you could just grab pen and paper and write it down.

Some ideas:

- a turning point in my career;
- a time I messed up;
- something that happened at school (or university).

After telling your story, go back and review your role in the story and the role of others. Can you tell the story in a different way? For example:

- From a different perspective, such as that of another character, or a neutral observer?
- By picking out different aspects of what happened?
- By starting or ending the story at a different point in time?
- By finding a different angle? For example, if you messed up a piece of work, did you tell yourself this is not your strength and have avoided that type of task? Or did you learn something specific that you were able to apply in different situations? When did you apply the learning? How did this change you?

Summary: Crafting your inner landscape

- Human beings use metaphorical images and language, with concepts and ideas related to more tangible sensory aspects of our physical experience.
- Recognizing how we use metaphor and story can help us to understand our own way of seeing the world, and how we make meaning from our experiences.
- Working with and changing our internal metaphors offers us the potential to change our experience of the external world.
- We can rewrite our stories from different perspectives, understanding that our story can be our truth. But where it constrains us, we can tell a different truth, remaining authentic but releasing or empowering ourselves.

Your perspective?

To what extent do you agree or disagree with the ideas in this chapter? What does this tell you about the way you see the world?

What are the metaphors and stories that you use to describe your career path and your current role at work?

Are there metaphors and stories from your past that you'd like to change?

In this chapter you've looked at how you create your unique experience of the world through the stories you tell yourself and the deep metaphors that underpin your experience. Your inner life is filled with stories, images, metaphors, and ways of seeing and interpreting what goes on around you. Deepening your understanding of your own inner landscape may open the door to a greater appreciation of the individuality of others.

In the next section, we shift our focus onto relationships with other people, with those that we meet and communicate with at work and in other parts of our lives. To understand others, we need the ability to listen to them both accurately and empathically, and so the next chapter explores listening as the foundation for connecting with others.

Dimension 2

Connecting With

I t's not every day that a workshop genuinely changes your life. But this time, it did.

I was 24 and having left formal education at 17, I wanted to get back into learning and booked onto a one-day acting workshop. I'd enjoyed being in plays at school, although my main recollection was trying to remember my lines and the feeling of nerves just before going on stage. I didn't really know what to expect from the workshop, but I'd always wanted to try acting again and thought it would build my confidence.

It was transformational. We started the day with some warmup exercises, connecting with ourselves, our bodies, and our voices. Looking back, the day was my first small taster of many of the skills covered in the previous section, which I went on to develop further through acting training, and then through professional-level training in counselling, coaching, and facilitation skills.

After the warmup, we moved on to acting, but there wasn't a script in sight. It turned out the day was about improvisation, working with others in the group to devise characters and short scenes. Now, the key with improvisation is that a scene will only work if you listen to what your partner says and build on their ideas. It's literally about interacting. You listen, and then respond. If you're too busy thinking about what you're going to say next, you lose that ability to respond, and it's the responsiveness that can create a little bit of magic as together you build a situation and a story.

In this section I'm sharing some of knowledge and skills that I've learnt over the past 30 years. These are ideas that I've found valuable when it comes to connecting with others, both personally and professionally. And of these, listening skills are absolutely the foundation for me. We can always get better at listening and I'm not pretending that I do it perfectly; there's always more to learn. But my listening skills are strong enough to underpin much of what I do for a living.

We'll also look at other aspects of interaction, such as: the use of questions, story, and metaphor, the importance of mutual respect, and the way you use your voice and body language. We'll also explore the subject of communication styles. I've discovered that understanding your preferred styles of communication and recognizing different styles can be a game changer. We also look at the importance of feedback, and how giving and receiving feedback can help you and others to develop and expand awareness.

The ideas described in this section draw on my professional certifications in different facilitation and communication methodologies, tracing back to a small spark lit through that introductory improvisation workshop. Participants in my training courses have found these ideas helpful and insightful. My hope is that you'll also find value in this section, some sparks to help you connect more deeply and communicate more clearly with the people in your life.

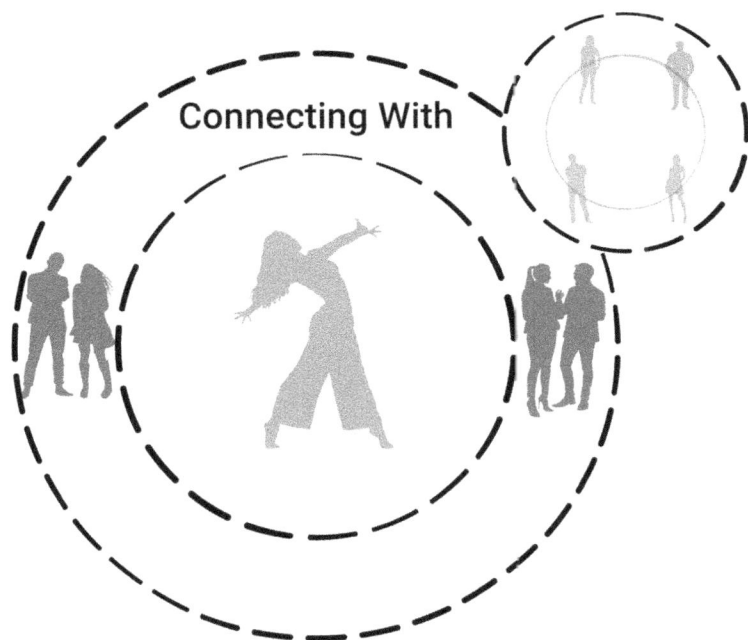

Connecting With

Chapter 6

I hear you
Listening as the master key to connection

The secret to better relationships

Imagine you could find a master key to unlocking deeper conversations and stronger relationships. A key that opens many doors. It can open a door to stronger personal and business relationships. It can help you to learn and grow. It can expand your thinking and understanding. It can even offer access to greater peace of mind.

I believe there is such a master key. And it's called listening. Listening is at the very heart of connection. Listening keeps two-way communication alive; it allows for the circulation and development of ideas between those involved in a conversation.

Yes, we also need to be able to speak well, and put our thoughts into words that are clear and that resonate with others. But if you can get the listening right, you'll find it's easier to find the words when it's your turn to speak.

In this chapter we'll look at why listening is important. We'll consider different levels of listening and explore ways to become a better listener.

Why is listening so important?

In personal and professional relationships, listening will help you understand and connect with others. In a meaningful conversation, you will stretch yourself imaginatively to understand how other people think and feel. And by extending your own imagination into the world of another person, you may find it easier to craft your words and tone of voice to communicate your perspective in a way that will resonate with them.

I find that the more and more I listen to people, through my coaching and facilitation work and in other conversations, the less and less I want to judge anyone. And the less judgemental I am, the more I'm able to make it safe for people to open up to me.

So, there's a virtuous circle created, where your listening helps people to connect and communicate with you, just as it helps you to communicate effectively with them.

In contrast, half-hearted listening can result in a sense of separation. You may find yourself responding less to what the other person has said and more to your own thoughts about what the other person has said. People won't feel so connected to you. They may feel misunderstood, and they may focus more on correcting you or restating their initial point than on moving a conversation forward with mutual understanding.

Listening is a skill that you can use to help anyone. If a friend is in distress, you can help just by listening. You can't necessarily solve other people's problems, but you can listen. Listening can be so powerful that charities such as the Samaritans and other helplines have saved lives purely through being there and listening at the end of a phone. Even on a phone call, there is a qualitative difference to the speaker's experience when you listen deeply rather than being distracted.

At work, listening is the basis of effective professional relation-ships. Listening helps you lead your team through better under-standing their needs and motivators, so you can encourage and help them to perform at their best. It helps you build positive relationships with co-workers, through understanding their priorities and the challenges they face. And it's invaluable in sales situations as you seek to understand your customers and find ways to help them.

Four levels of listening

You can think about listening as having four levels. The differ-ence between the levels is ultimately the extent to which we focus our attention. At the first level, our attention is mainly with ourselves, and as we go down through the levels we focus more of our attention on the other person.

Level 1: Superficial listening

At this level, there is not much listening going on at all. Yes, you may be nodding and saying yes, but your attention is really on something else. Your attention may be with your own thoughts or on something else going on. It's as if the other person is in the background. You may also find that you're tuning the person in and out.

Let's be honest, most of us listen superficially at times. And for the person speaking, it's usually quite easy to sense when somebody is listening in this way. In fact, it can be surprisingly difficult to talk and communicate with somebody who isn't listening to us. Sometimes in training courses I run an exercise where one person is asked to speak for a few minutes on a topic of their choice, and the other person is asked to listen first with full attention and then to deliberately not listen. It's striking

how often people say that it's difficult to keep going and articulate their thoughts when their partner stops listening. We can
help or hinder other people's thinking through the extent to
which we are able to listen to them.[32]

The impact of superficial listening can clearly be detrimental at
work. If you're a manager or team leader and you don't listen
to your staff, then you are potentially hindering them from
doing a good job. Listening to people articulate their thoughts
and concerns is a way of supporting them to solve their own
problems. And it shows interest and respect for others to allow
for connection, whether that's in a professional context or with
family and friends.

Level 2: Conversational listening

The second level is a common everyday form of listening that
I call conversational listening. This is characterized by a back-
and-forward pattern of exchange.[33]

You'll be very familiar with this pattern. For example, I may
be talking about my holiday and say something like: 'We've
just been back from Tenerife and we did this and that', and the
other person might say 'How lovely, where did you stay?' And
you respond. And then the other person in this sort of conversation might come in with their own story. 'Oh yes, we've been
to the Canaries too; we stayed in Lanzarote...'

So, it's back and forth. You are hearing what the other person
is saying, but you're also coming in quite quickly with your
own experiences or views. Often in conversations, you'll see
a pattern of people exchanging their own stories or perspectives on a similar topic. They use the other person's contribution mainly as a jumping-off point to talk about their own
experiences.

To be clear, there's nothing wrong with this level of listening for day-to-day small talk and social conversations. It provides a comfortable level of connection with people who you may not know well or that you meet casually. And there is evidence that casual interactions are important to our sense of connection. Conversation is also a pleasant way to spend time and reconnect with friends. It offers a set of unspoken rules that help us to connect on a social level with topics that are easy to discuss. The weather, sports, television, theatre, or local events fall into these categories.

Conversational listening can also smooth the way to deeper levels of listening with people that you'd like to connect with more deeply. But if you only ever communicate at the conversational level, you miss out on opportunities to understand both yourself and others in a more profound way.

In a professional setting, conversational listening may be enough for simple communication, such as the allocation of familiar day-to-day tasks and for social interactions at work. But this level of listening may be insufficient in management or team-working situations. For example, helping people perform at work may involve deeper conversations about internal barriers to action, improving working relationships, and achieving goals.

Level 3: Active listening

Here, you, as the listener, are more focused and attentive to what the other person is saying than at previous levels. You may also be more aware of what they are not saying. And you will be noticing how they speak, picking up on emotions and body language as well as words. This is the level of empathic listening, where we try to metaphorically put ourselves in someone else's shoes and to really understand their perspective, both thoughts and feelings.

It requires an active focus of our attention on the other person. Active listening is sometimes taught through a set of techniques. These techniques may include:

- reflecting, which means repeating back some of the other person's words, which shows we've heard them and are encouraging them to continue;
- paraphrasing or summarizing what somebody has said to check our understanding is correct;
- using encouraging sounds such as 'mmm', or words such as 'yes' and 'go on';
- using body language to show our interest, for example nodding or leaning forward.

These techniques can all be helpful to the speaker. But active listening isn't primarily a question of using active listening techniques. It's primarily about our intention to keep more of our focus on the other person. We listen actively when we give someone our full attention and remain interested in what they have to say. We can bring a gentle curiosity to our listening, allowing ourselves to be more interested in what the other person is saying than in what we are going to say next.

Level 4: Deep listening

Deep listening is at a level you could expect from a trained listener, such as a counsellor or coach. The focus here stays on the speaker, often for an extended time. As much of your attention as possible is on what the other person says. Your attention is fully focused on trying to understand them, their words, and the feelings behind the words. On what is being said and what is not being said. And on how it's being said. You will also be picking up messages that come through the intonation, gesture, pauses, and rhythm of the speaker, and metaphorically going with them on a journey as you provide a space for people to think.

In deep listening, you are unlikely to be saying much at all. This is partly because of the way deep listening can support another person to think more deeply, and therefore need less by way of prompts or questions. Nancy Kline is an expert in ways that we can support and encourage other people's thinking, and she emphasizes the generative quality of our attention. 'Attention is an act of creation. It *generates* thinking in another person'.[34] And rather than jumping in when there is a pause in the conversation, you are likely to hold back before intervening. You are giving people time to connect with the flow of their own thoughts and feelings, and being there for them.

Your energy is focused on trying to understand the world from the other person's perspective and to connect with their thoughts, feelings, and experience. If you do speak, it may be to reflect back a few words that seem important or have an emotional charge. And any questions you ask will be designed to help them go deeper into their thinking, rather than giving your views. We look at questions in detail in Chapter 8.

Some people find this level of listening comes naturally, but for many of us, listening for an extended period at this level is not easy to do. But this doesn't mean we don't have the potential within us to listen deeply. Being engrossed in a fascinating story from a master storyteller is an example of when our attention can be fully engaged, in a way that may feel effortless. And above all, listening is a learnable skill that we can practise and improve.

If you are a coach or counsellor, then the ability to listen deeply is a core skill and one of the most valuable ways to support your clients. In leadership, the ability to take this deep listening role from time to time will help you to develop and grow your people, for example by giving them time and space to think through a problem for themselves rather than trying to solve it for them. And with family and friends, it will help you to support people when they really need someone to talk to by giving them the gift of time and sustained attention.

Carl Rogers and the core conditions

An experience that helped me learn the art of listening was completing the first year of a BA degree in Person Centred Counselling. This course offered a deep dive into counselling psychologist Carl Rogers' 'core conditions'.[35] The core conditions as taught to counsellors are:

- empathy (trying to see the world through the other person's eyes);
- congruence (being genuine and present with the other person and aware of your own responses);
- unconditional positive regard (listening with warmth, with acceptance, and without judgement).

The course had a big impact on me. As well as helping me to develop listening skills, it also gave me an experience of extended group work. The group work allowed us ample time to reflect out loud in a group, in the presence of quality listening from others. This experience helped me to learn and appreciate myself and others in a way I hadn't before. It also sparked a longstanding interest in facilitation and group process.

The core conditions allow for deep listening. You are doing your best to see the world from the other person's perspective, which is empathy. Empathy is not the same as sympathy. It's not the same as feeling sorry for the person, or feeling angry on their behalf, or even feeling happy for them. It's about understanding what it is that they are feeling.

Empathy can't happen if you are judging the other person. This doesn't mean you need to agree with their perspective, only that you are trying to understand it. In fact, approval is a judgement, as much as condemnation is.

Unconditional positive regard allows you to accept that what the other person is expressing is true for them. It is about holding a respect for the other person's humanity, accepting them as they are.

And congruence is about being aware of yourself and your own reactions. It's an ability to notice the impact of the conversation on your own mind and body, whilst still being able to return your deep attention to the other person.

As Carl Rogers explains in *A Way of Being*:

> To be with another in this [empathic] way means that for the time being, you lay aside your own views and values in order to enter another's world without prejudice. In some sense it means that you lay aside your self; this can only be done by persons who are secure enough in themselves that they know they will not get lost in what may turn out to be the strange or bizarre world of the other, and that they can comfortably return to their own world when they wish.[36]

As Rogers suggests, it is difficult to be truly empathic and accepting unless you have a strong enough sense of connection with yourself to be able to listen deeply to others and enter their reality without getting lost in it. This is one reason why connecting within provides such an important foundation for deeper connection with another person.

And when we are more able to connect more with our observing self, as described in Chapter 4, it is easier for us to practise unconditional positive regard. We can listen from the perspective of a gentle observer rather than getting caught up in judgements. And when we are identified with this part of ourselves, we can be congruent or, to use another word, genuine in our listening. We are congruent because we are genuinely not judging the other person, and if we notice judgement creeping in from time to time, then we can choose not to go down that line of thinking.

Getting better at listening

Most of us could probably become even better listeners, whatever our current skill level. And for most of us, there are probably situations and times when our listening could be better. For example, I'm better during the daytime than evening. And I can find listening easier in a work situation than at home.

Active listening is for the most part an appropriate level for worthwhile connection, as you develop your ability to become more and more able to listen deeply without losing your sense of self.

Listening actively and at times deeply is powerful and valuable. But is it easy? I suspect the honest answer is 'not always'. I say that as someone who is a trained and experienced listener, but who is still far from perfect and notice myself jumping in a bit too soon. Here are some tips and ideas that I personally find helpful, and I hope you will too.

Intention

One of the most powerful ways to improve your listening skill is simply to make a conscious decision that you will listen. Try it, and notice what happens when you enter into a conversation with a clear intention that you will listen.

This means listening with no ulterior motives. For example, it's not about trying to listen so you can then persuade the other of your point of view; there's no agenda beyond hearing the other person.

Relax your body

When we are relaxed and at ease, other people will pick up on our body language and relax too. Imagine what it's like to try and articulate a difficult thought with someone hovering over you with tense muscles and impatient gestures. Then imagine someone who is relaxed and appearing to have plenty of time. How will this make you feel?

Soft eye contact

Look at the other person; then allow your gaze to soften so you are looking at them in the wider context of their surroundings. There is a difference between gentle eye contact and staring. If you allow your field of vision to expand, this will help you to relax and listen well.

Allow silence

When someone has finished, hold back from rushing in with your thoughts, particularly if they look as though they might still be thinking.

Gentle curiosity

Listen with a gentle sense of curiosity and interest. The curiosity is about the other person. How do they see the world? What do they think or feel?

If I find myself drifting in my own thoughts or opinions as someone is speaking, I simply encourage myself to refocus by asking myself: 'I wonder where they are going with their thinking?'

Allow yourself to become increasingly interested in the other person and what they have to say. Get gently curious about what they will say next. Ask yourself: 'where are they going with this?' And respond spontaneously to what you hear.

Ask questions that encourage the person to think more deeply

We'll explore questions in the next chapter. The point I want to make here is to not jump in too quickly with questions; instead allow people to follow their own train of thought. And when you do ask a question, make it helpful to the other person rather than to satisfy your own desire to know more. So you might ask a question to encourage the other person to deepen or broaden their thinking. But when listening, be wary of asking questions that come from your own agenda instead of building on the speaker's own thinking.

Intentional practice

Honing your listening skills takes practice and reflection. The chances are that you have multiple opportunities to practise. Listen to friends, family, and colleagues. If you feel you lack social connection in your life, look for ways to expand your network. There is more on this in Chapter 12.

In relationships that really matter to you, can you listen for 10 minutes, 20 minutes, 30 minutes, an hour, if necessary? Listening will do more to transform your relationship than just about anything else. Ask a friend or partner if you can each take 10 minutes to just listen to each other, not trying to help or change anything for each other. Just to listen, witness, and hear.

Relax into the process

A final thought about listening – it can be relaxing. If you're really listening to someone, you need to temporarily stop thinking about your own worries or concerns. I'm an advocate of mindfulness and meditation practices, which can help you become more aware of your own inner dialogue and distractions. And I also find that listening is an example of mindfulness in practice. When I relax and gently bring the focus of my attention onto someone else, it gives me a break from myself!

In conclusion, I encourage you to set an intention to listen more deeply to someone today, to relax, soften your eye contact, and stay interested in what the person is thinking and feeling, and what they might say next.

Practices

Soft eye contact

You can practise this by just choosing to look at an object, say a tree or a picture. Continue to look at the object, whilst softening and expanding your gaze so that you are taking in the person, or the object, within its surroundings. Relax into this soft gaze so that when you're listening to someone, you can comfortably maintain eye contact without staring.

Empathic perspective taking

An exercise to help build empathy is to listen to someone that you would normally disagree with and try to see the world from their perspective. This doesn't need to be in person; it could be an interview with someone on TV, video or radio. Practise putting yourself in their shoes. You may sometimes notice that your attention has moved away from their perspective, and instead you are noticing the impact they have on you, e.g. do you feel any anger or irritation? If that happens, acknowledge that your attention has wandered and gently bring your focus back to the speaker.

Another way to build empathy can be to read fiction, particularly character-driven novels. Through the magic of words, you can enter into the minds of very different people, such as the amoral Tom Ripley created by Patricia Highsmith, or the infatuated Emma Bovary, in Flaubert's eponymous masterpiece.

One more question

Next time you're in a conversation and notice you're about to give your view, try holding back. Instead, ask one more question about how the other person is thinking or feeling.

Summary: Crafting listening

- Listening is the key to connection, and a powerful starting point is setting an intention to listen well.
- Active and deep listening require you to give your attention to what the other person is saying. If you notice that you are distracted by your own thoughts and reactions, use this as a cue to gently return your attention to the other person.
- Remain gently curious about the other person and about what they are going to say next.

Your perspective?

How easy do you find it to put yourself in someone else's shoes?

What distracts you or gets in the way of listening well?

How might improving your listening skills help you at work? Or with family and friends?

What one change could you make to improve your ability to listen?

In this chapter you've considered why listening is important for connection, the different levels of listening, and ways to develop your listening skills.

We'll now move on to thinking about how we communicate our point of view in a way that allows us to be heard, whilst maintaining connection and showing respect for both ourselves and others.

Chapter 7

I would like to be heard The skills of assertive and respectful communication

'Someone who is assertive behaves confidently and is not frightened to say what they want or believe.' Cambridge Dictionary definition.[37]

Do you ever feel that your communication could have more impact? That your views and preferences aren't taken as seriously as they could be?

Assertive communication means that you express yourself clearly, so that you are heard. And, crucially, it is based on respect. This means respect for both yourself and the other person. You are both equally important and valuable, and you both have the right to be heard. This mutuality is the foundation of assertive communication.

In this chapter we look at ways to become more assertive. We'll also consider different communication styles, and how we can adapt our communication to connect more effectively with people who are different to us.

Assertion is not aggression

To be clear, assertive behaviour is not the same as aggressive behaviour.

Thinking that you're always right is not assertiveness. Forcing your views on others is aggressive behaviour. Dominating a conversation is aggressive behaviour. This may show up as someone who talks for too long, or interrupts other people, or continually shifts the conversation back to their agenda. Does your heart sink when you hear the same person talking yet again at a meeting and not showing interest in anyone else's views? This behaviour is not assertiveness.

Having the courage to say what you really think, and feel, is assertive.

Be clear about what you think and feel

Assertive communication starts with clarity about what you want to communicate. What do you want and need? And how can you express your thoughts and feelings in a way that respects other people and their perspectives, wants, and needs?

Respecting others is important. And equally important is self-respect. If you don't feel that your views are valid or that you have anything worth saying or sharing, this can lead to a passive style of communication. As can a belief that you are not someone worth listening to.

If you find you're always the one who gives in, to let other people have their own way, then this can lead to resentment and a further loss of self-esteem. It can also result in passive-aggressive behaviours such as gossiping about people behind their backs because you haven't had the courage to speak to them directly.

Own your perspective

You have a right to express what you think and feel. Your feelings are always valid. But to be assertive, you need to understand the importance of owning your perspective.

This means sharing what we think, or feel, or would like to happen, using 'I' statements, such as: 'I think…', 'I feel…', 'I would like…'

If you disagree with someone, it helps to acknowledge you've heard and understood their point of view. You might then introduce your views with a phrase like: 'I have a different perspective…'

If the other person doesn't seem to have heard or understood, repeat your message in a different way. Try varying the wording to see what resonates with the other person. Adjust your language but keep the core message unchanged until you're sure you've been heard.

Be respectful of other views

Everyone sees the world differently – it couldn't be otherwise. Everything we see and hear reaches us through our sensory and nervous system and is recreated internally in the physical structure of our brain. Realizing this may help us to bring the quality of gentle curiosity to our listening. And it may remind us to listen with greater compassion and the willingness to put ourselves in someone else's position.

We've talked about how the foundation of good communication is to listen carefully to other perspectives. Listen to understand; not to either agree or disagree, but instead to discover what the other person thinks. Stay interested in their point of view and keep an open mind; is there something they've said that might shift your viewpoint?

And demonstrate that you understand the other person's perspective. You may wish to reflect back some of their key words or summarize what they have said in your own words to check that you've understood. Ask questions that encourage the other person to tell you more about what they think and to check your understanding. If your attention wanders when someone is speaking, be honest about this. Ask them to repeat what you've missed.

Build on what others are saying: 'And...' phrasing

The use of the word 'and' can help you communicate assertively without being confrontational. You can acknowledge someone's viewpoint and then put your views forward without negating the other's perspective. For example:

> *'I understand that you find this frustratingly bureaucratic. And I have a different perspective, in that it helps us keep ongoing records and prevents issues down the line.'*

This can be less confrontational than the word 'but'. Compare these two responses:

> *'I know you have a lot of priorities to juggle. But this report must be finished today.'*

> *'I know you have a lot of priorities to juggle. And this report must be finished today.'*

The work 'but' tends to cancel out the previous sentence, whereas the word 'and' builds on it. 'And' acknowledges the reality of the other, whilst allowing you to also present your view.

Clearly there are times that you might choose to use the word 'but'. I would encourage you to think carefully before you use it to ensure it doesn't come over as dismissive of the other person.

Notice when you're projecting your thoughts and feelings onto others

I'm sure you've experienced situations where someone's words or behaviours have triggered a negative response in you. You may consider them rude or ill-informed or dishonest, for example. In some instances, a negative response may be fully justified. On other occasions it may be that you have made assumptions, for example about someone's intentions. Or it may be that someone has touched on an area where you have personal insecurities or sensitivities. We all have our personal trigger points to which we tend to react emotionally rather than rationally.

Say, for instance, that you feel another person's behaviour was disrespectful in some way and needs to be challenged. If so, then challenge assertively, for example by saying: 'When you interrupted me, I felt unheard and was less willing to give my full attention to your point of view'. You are linking the other person's behaviour with your reaction, whilst taking responsibility for how you have reacted.

Accusations are not assertive. When you project your negative feelings or thoughts onto other people, this tends to come over as aggressive. Contrast saying: 'you're rude' versus: 'I would like to have time to finish my point before you come in with your perspective'.

It can be helpful to realize that people can react very differently to what might be perceived as aggressive behaviour. For example, someone might say: 'When you told me to shut up, I was wondering if you were feeling criticized or overwhelmed?' The listener in this example may not have been triggered into a negative response, whereas another listener might have been offended or upset by what could have been seen as rude or discourteous words.

You always have the power to choose how you respond to others. In words attributed to Eleanor Roosevelt: 'No one can make you feel inferior without your consent'.[38]

I don't in any way condone bullying or aggressive behaviour. This is not acceptable and when it takes place, we need to call it out. And there are many instances where we may jump to conclusions about someone's intention. We may assume that the other person meant to be harsh or critical, but this wasn't their aim. An assertive response may lead to a more honest and deeper relationship, whether that's in a personal or professional context.

Explore your own barriers to being assertive

Communication techniques can help to grow your confidence in behaving assertively. And there is also value in digging a little deeper to examine the reasons why you sometimes struggle to be assertive.

Is this because, at some level, you don't believe you're as good as other people? This belief sometimes underlies passive behaviour. Conversely, this underlying belief can lead to aggressive behaviour. Maybe you feel, at some level, that you must be forceful to be heard?

Or do you judge some people as not truly worthy of respect? Maybe because of their education level, or even their race or gender. Some of these judgements can be hard to recognize.

The term 'unconscious bias' describes judgements that exist below our level of conscious awareness. If you become aware that you feel more anxious going into conversations with some people than others, it's worth taking time to reflect honestly on this. Are there any patterns that could reflect fears or prejudices below your level of awareness? Once you become aware of an assumption or bias, it's much easier to consciously decide to overcome it.

Assertiveness is also related to the ability to identify and set personal boundaries. What is ok and not ok for you? There are many areas where you might like to reflect on your boundaries, such as: your time; physical contact; the way you like to be spoken to; your ethical no-go areas. And how can you communicate these boundaries clearly and respectfully? This comes around again to the importance of becoming clear about the answers yourself, so that you can communicate effectively with others through your words and actions.

The paradox of caring and not caring

There are paradoxes in connecting in a way that is truly authentic and respectful.

You need to care about the other person. And you also need to not care too much about what the other person thinks of you.

You need to be able to speak what you see as your truth. And you also need to accept that there are other ways of seeing, and to allow yourself to perhaps be changed by another.

You need to be able to stay centred and connected with your own physicality, thoughts, and emotions. And yet remain open to being affected by another person, with empathy and compassion.

Acceptance

Recognizing and accepting your own thoughts and feelings allows you to build bridges with other people. How do you respond when someone criticizes you or says something that challenges your self-image? What if someone makes a remark that triggers difficult feelings within you? By noticing your own reactions, you can more easily stay in relationship with another person.

Sometimes you may need to metaphorically 'park' your observation and explore it later to work out what was happening in your body and mind in response to a trigger, for example if something happens at work. Treat your own response with interest and curiosity: 'what's that about?'

When we take responsibility for our own inner world, it's easier to let go of a desire to control other people. We can let them be themselves and choose an attitude of acceptance and interest, rather than resistance and judgement.

Compassion in communication

The Latin source of the word compassion means 'to suffer with'. When we feel compassion for someone, we recognize our common humanity. Compassion can be difficult as it involves opening up to someone else's emotional or physical pain, and it may trigger difficult feelings for us. In connecting and empathizing with other people, we will at times find ourselves connecting with their pain. It's important to be able to care, but also to be aware of the risk of compassion fatigue, and that if our caring becomes overwhelming, we need to take care of ourselves. It's not selfish; we need kindness as much as anyone else.

Influencing without coercion

There are times in a conversation where you are trying to influence another person, whether that's to agree with your choice of restaurant for dinner, or to take on a piece of work, or to spend a large sum of money on a car.

There's nothing wrong with putting your case in a way that's assertive, passionate, evidence based, and persuasive. But legitimate influence can move into coercion if you try and pressurize, fool, or manipulate other people. Stay open to signs of someone's discomfort and adjust your approach if you can see someone is uncomfortable. What's going on for them? Do you need to give them space, back off? Have you moved away from dialogue in an attempt to get your view across?

If communication shifts into coercion, then the essence of mutual respect is lost and connection can shift into manipulation. Even if we can get away with this initially, there is likely to be a longer-term detrimental effect on the relationship. An example is 'buyer's remorse', when we feel we've been talked into saying yes to something that, on reflection, was not right for us.

Communication styles

We all have our own natural communication styles and preferences. Do you tend to be quite direct and find yourself irritated by people who take ages to get to the point? Do you need to feel you're in a safe environment and that you won't be put down or ridiculed before you speak out? Do you believe you need to have all the facts and details at your fingertips before you express your opinion? Do you enjoy the limelight and attention of others, but find it harder to listen patiently?

Differences in communication style can have a negative impact on our sense of connection. We may feel more comfortable with people who share our style, for example. Understanding the preferred communication styles of ourselves and others can make it easier for us to appreciate our differences and to adapt our style where necessary to enhance connection and mutual understanding.

DISC

DISC is one of my favourite models for analysing communication styles. It helps you to understand and recognize your own communication style and preferences, and to appreciate how these might differ from those of other people.

The model comes from the work of psychologist William Moulton Marston, who identified four behavioural styles: Dominance, Inducement, Submission, and Compliance. Modern interpretations use a variety of labels to describe each style, and the image below shows commonly used terms.

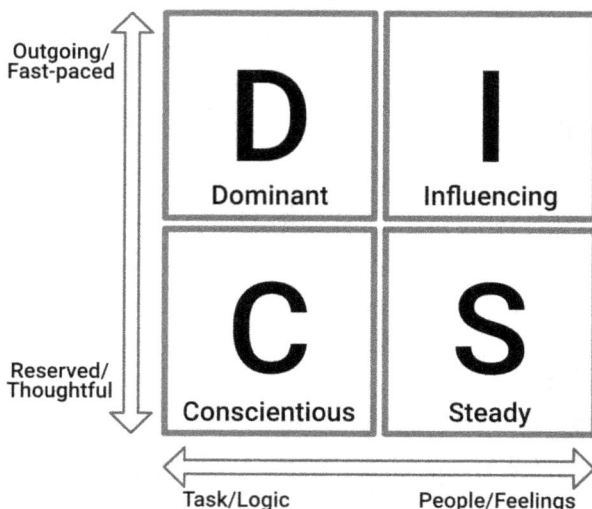

Outgoing/Fast-paced

Reserved/Thoughtful

D — Dominant

I — Influencing

C — Conscientious

S — Steady

Task/Logic   People/Feelings

DISC is plotted on two axes, considering two aspects of our behaviour. The first axis looks at how outgoing and fast-paced we are, versus how reserved and thoughtful. The second axis looks at the extent to which we are task and logic focused, versus people and feelings focused.

Like all models, it's a simplification. But by simplifying the complexity that is human communication, it helps us to navigate our way through potential miscommunication and misunderstandings that are down to differences in style.

There are several validated DISC questionnaires which will give you a much deeper and more nuanced understanding of your own style and how to relate to others. But one of the reasons I like DISC is that the basic framework is straightforward. It will allow you to start to identify your preferred style so that you can use the model in a practical way, as a guide to being flexible in your communication.

Be aware that although you can use this model to infer other people's style, it's important to keep an open mind. It's not always possible to identify someone's natural preferences from what you observe. People can, and do, adapt their behaviour, for example to fit a workplace culture or the expectations of their role. We can all choose to behave in each of the four styles. A good communicator will be able to adapt their style appropriately for the situation.

Overview of DISC styles

This is a basic overview of the four styles, including some of the adjectives that are used to describe key behaviours of each type.

Where do you think you sit?

D style (dominant, direct, driving)

Ds communicate in a way that is direct and to the point. They don't like waffle or rambling narratives. At their most extreme or when under pressure, Ds will dispense with social niceties. Because they are so direct, Ds can come across as abrupt or even rude. Their communication style has the benefit of clarity.

If you are communicating with a D, be direct. Think through the message you want to communicate, as they may lack patience to listen to you thinking things through out loud, particularly if they are under pressure.

I style (influencing, inspirational, interactive)

People with an I preference are outgoing and people oriented. They like to speak and to think out loud. I styles are often good at presenting and persuading. They can be enthusiastic and energetic communicators. I-style communication tends to focus more on the big picture, rather than the fine detail.

If you are communicating with an I style, don't talk at them for long periods. Ask them questions, encourage them to talk and communicate. People with an I communication style like to be actively engaged in conversation. I styles usually enjoy positive feedback and appreciation (and can be susceptible to flattery).

S style (steady, supportive, stable)

People with an S style are people oriented and tend to be more reserved. They are interested in people and often make good listeners. They don't like to be put on the spot and often prefer to have time to think about things before responding.

I would like to be heard   115

In communicating with an S, ensure they are given space to be heard. People with an S style may appreciate time to reflect on a question or to talk it through with one other person before speaking out in a bigger group. They will tend to be interested in the impact that ideas have on the people involved.

Social conversation openers are important to S styles, for example asking them how they are, asking after their loved one, or showing an interest in their weekend.

C style (conscientious, cautious, critical thinking)

Cs are reserved and task focused. They tend to be detail oriented and sometimes risk averse. C-style communicators will often go into a lot of detail about their subject. They tend to think before speaking.

If you're communicating with a C, then make sure you have researched your subject and can back up what you're saying. C styles don't respond well to pressure; give them time to think about a question rather than pushing them for a quick response.

Using DISC to troubleshoot miscommunication

DISC can help you to see where a communication problem may be down to a difference in style. A style mismatch isn't always the reason for miscommunication, but it can make communication harder, and it's certainly worth considering when you're trying to improve interactions.

Mismatched styles are most pronounced across the diagonal of the model. If your style is I (influence), with a tendency to enthusiastic, big-picture communication, you may find it harder to engage a C (conscientious) who is more concerned with the detail. They may feel you lack authority or rigour.

And a C-style communicator may be speaking to an I and find the latter has switched off. They are bored or lost in the detail. They would like to have heard the key points and then be asked to give their perspective. They would have appreciated the opportunity to ask questions or talk through the implications.

With a D (direct) and S (steady) communication, someone with a D style may come over as intimidating to an S style; the latter often need to build a relationship before they feel comfortable sharing their perspective, and they may need more time to think. Ds may experience the S communication style as wasting time on the 'soft stuff' and not getting to the point quickly enough.

My predominant styles are I and S, and I'm married to someone whose predominant style is D. I've adjusted to, and appreciate, my husband's direct style of communication although it took a while. And we've had numerous exchanges where I talk expansively around a request, bringing in background information and emotions, for example. And he then asks me to please just come out directly with what I want.

Bear in mind that it can be harder work to communicate in a style that comes less naturally to you; it requires a greater investment of energy. If you're naturally reserved, you're not going to suddenly become a raging extrovert, for example. But you can identify situations where you do need to be more assertive and plan for how you will adapt your communication where needed. And conversely if you're naturally direct in your style, you may need to hold back and allow the other person more time than you might ideally prefer.

Although it can be easier to communicate with some people than others, this doesn't mean that you can't connect effectively with those who have a different approach. Appreciating differences, and being willing to adapt your style, will help you to bridge gaps in understanding and connection.

Skills for difficult conversations

Many communication issues come down to differences in style, or values, or priorities, or perspectives, or assumptions. And the following skills and behaviours will help:

- Listening carefully, as discussed in Chapter 6. This provides the basis for understanding. It allows you to identify what is important to them and how they see the situation.
- Asking questions to check understanding. There is more on this in Chapter 8.
- Be clear about your perspective, think carefully about your key messages, and communicate your views calmly and assertively.
- Maintain your respect for the person as an individual, whilst stating your views clearly using 'I' statements.
- Avoid accusations and inferences about others' motives.
- Adapt your communication style so it's aligned with the other person's, which may mean being more direct, more detail oriented, or more conversational.
- Stay open to changing your mind if the facts change.
- Be open to finding common ground. Look for areas of agreement to build on. Or if that's not possible, agree to differ, whilst retaining respect and courtesy for the other.
- Look for opportunities to express genuine appreciation for the other person.

Dealing with pressure

There are some situations where you become aware that the other person is trying to influence you in a way that goes beyond simply sharing their perspective.

You may feel that someone is attacking you personally; making accusations that you feel you need to defend; undermining you with sarcasm; or bullying, which is never acceptable. It may be that you feel that you are being put under pressure to purchase something or make an immediate decision. If you find yourself in this position, here are some tips on how to manage it.

- Firstly, find a way to connect back with yourself. Being at the receiving end of aggressive or passive-aggressive behaviour can leave you feeling off-centre. Take a couple of breaths. Feel your feet on the floor.
- If you feel uncomfortable, excuse yourself from the situation if appropriate, so you can give yourself some thinking time.
- Don't be pushed into a quick decision (e.g. pressure sales). Say that you want some time to think about it.
- Do your best to keep your voice steady and calm. Be prepared to repeat yourself if necessary, and use 'I' statements: 'I will take time to think about it', 'I won't give a decision now; I will let you have my decision later'. The word 'won't' rather than 'can't' gives you more control. Someone may try to persuade you that you 'can' do something. But it's in your control as to whether you 'will'.
- Don't get drawn into an argument. Or feel that you have to answer questions. Sometimes the most powerful response is to say nothing. Allow silence.

Summary: Crafting assertiveness and respect

- Assertive communication involves respect for both yourself and other people. You have a right to say what you really think and feel. And so does the other person.
- Becoming more aware of your own reactions will give you more choices over how you respond to others.
- Using 'I' statements helps you to express and own your thoughts and feelings, rather than projecting them onto the other person.
- Different communication styles can lead to misunderstandings. Get to know your preferred styles and learn to recognize other people's styles. Adapting your style will help you to get your message across more clearly.

Your perspective?

How easy do you find it to express your views clearly, even if it involves disagreeing with others?

What practices could help you stay calm and centred in difficult conversations?

How can you best prepare for a potentially difficult conversation?

What is your natural communication style?

What specifically can you do to adapt your style where needed?

In this chapter you looked at the importance of speaking clearly and assertively, maintaining equal respect for yourself and others. You also considered your communication style preferences, and how adapting your communication style can help you connect with a wider range of people.

In the next chapter, we'll drill down into the skill of asking questions in a way that helps us to understand and connect more deeply with other people.

Chapter 8

What do you really think? Using questions to deepen connection and understanding

What happens when you ask a question?

In reading this sub-heading, what is going through your mind?

Are you starting to think of an answer?

As we've explored, listening with respect is the starting point for connection and a springboard to meaningful conversations. It's the foundation for dialogues where all those involved stretch and extend their understanding of each other and the subject being discussed. And a valuable tool for deepening connection is asking great questions. Listening underpins good questioning, as good-quality questions arise from what you're hearing and observing in the other person.

Your skill with questions is not dependent on how many questions you ask; instead, it's about what you ask and how you phrase your question. Find questions that help other people to think more clearly and which help to deepen or expand their thinking. When you're listening deeply, you may not need to ask many questions. This is because empathic listening supports quality thinking.

Deepening your understanding of questions and how to use them will help you pose better questions, more of the time. Having said that, there's no one perfect question that will guarantee you a thoughtful reply. You may ask what, on the surface, seems a great question, yet it doesn't resonate with the other person. If this happens, ask a different question.

In this chapter we'll start with an overview of different types of question and go on to explore some specific questioning techniques, and how and when to use them.

Open and closed questions

It's likely that you are aware of the difference between open and closed questions.

Open questions allow the other person to answer in the way that they choose. For example:

'How do you like to spend your weekends?'

'What would be your ideal career?'

'What would you like to have happen?'

The value of asking open questions is that they allow the other person to express themselves however they choose in their response. Rather than making assumptions about what the other person thinks or feels, you open the door to hearing what they really think and feel, which encourages a more authentic level of connection.

Closed questions invite a specific response. This may be a 'yes or no' response, or it may be a limited choice between specified options. For example:

'Are you free to meet on Tuesday next week?'

'Shall we meet on Tuesday or Wednesday?'

Closed questions are useful to confirm your understanding:

'Am I right in thinking that…?'

And they are useful towards the end of a conversation:

'Have we covered everything?'

'When are you planning to complete that?'

Leading questions

It can be difficult to ask truly open questions, even when you understand the concept. It's very easy to fall into the trap of asking leading questions (as in 'leading the witness').

Leading questions may be statements or specific suggestions, disguised as questions. They could be in the form of either closed or open questions, as in the following examples:

'Have you thought of asking Jane for advice?' (closed/ leading)

'How are you going to ask Jane for advice?' (open/ leading)

The problem with leading questions is that they can limit the space for other people to respond, and potentially put barriers in the way of open communication and genuine connection. If you do want to suggest a way forward, it might be better to do this more openly, maybe just by asking 'may I make a suggestion?'

Probing questions

Probing questions are those which probe for more details and specifics. For example:

'What specifically are you unhappy about?'

'What exactly did she say?'

These questions can help to deepen understanding on both sides. For example, in a management or coaching situation, they may help someone to understand and articulate how they think and feel about something.

The risk of asking too many probing questions is that they may be experienced as an interrogation. It's always worth asking yourself about the purpose behind your question. Is it to satisfy your own desire to hear their answer? Or is it because you're picking up a lack of clarity in what the other person is saying and believe a question could help them to clarify or deepen their own thinking.

Multiple questions

What happens when you ask too many questions at once? Does it make it easier for the other person to respond? Or can it cause some confusion? Which question do you want them to answer first? Did you have a purpose in asking multiple questions, or were you just not sure what to ask?

If you found the above paragraph disorientating, then hopefully my point is made. Multiple questions can confuse. Which question do you answer first? You may forget one or more of the questions. Or decide to ignore the ones that seem challenging or difficult to answer.

For clarity, ask one question at a time. Or if you choose to ask more than one question, ensure they are logically linked. Sometimes it makes sense to group a closed and open question together. To give a straightforward example: 'Did you go to the performance? If so, what did you think about it?'

Presuppositions

Presuppositions are underlying assumptions which are built into questions (or statements). The questions *presuppose* something is true and can therefore have the effect of funnelling replies in a certain direction, potentially limiting the other person's thinking or the range of responses that they may feel able to make. To connect effectively with someone else, we need to be aware of the extent to which our questions are pushing them in a particular direction. Understanding the impact of presuppositions can help us to phrase more effective questions.

Presuppositions can easily sneak into questions which seem quite open on the surface. For example: 'what are you enjoying about this book?' presupposes that you are enjoying it. That may or may not be true, although of course I hope that if you've read this far, you are at least finding something of interest in these pages.

Sometimes we use these presuppositions deliberately because we want to frame a situation in a certain way. I might ask my daughter 'what's your proudest achievement at school this week?', presupposing that there's something she is proud of or has achieved, and to encourage her to share it. A more open question might be: 'what was your experience at school this week?'

Presuppositions can also be used to manipulate someone into thinking they have limited choices. In sales, there is an approach called the alternative close where you presuppose someone will be making a purchase, and you therefore offer them a choice between this and that:

'Would you prefer the red or the blue option?'

'Are you going for the standard or deluxe package?'

Clearly there are times when people may choose to incorporate presuppositions. And it's helpful to look out for presuppositions in questions and be prepared to challenge underpinning assumptions where they don't serve you.

And when you're asking questions, be mindful of the use of presuppositions. Sometimes they are helpful and valid; for example when we presuppose that there is a solution to a problem, then this can help us to identify possible options and ways forward.

'What options do we have in this situation?'

'How can we get around this obstacle?'

There are also times in communication where it's important to avoid presuppositions. For example, if you want to learn what someone really thinks and feels, it's helpful to keep your questions as genuinely open as possible. This increases the chance that you'll learn something new. There is even a specific set of questions that have been developed to help eliminate presuppositions, as far as possible. These are known as Clean Language questions, and we'll explore them a little later in this chapter.

Why, what, where, when, who, and how

Most questions start with one of these six words, although not always. Questions can be communicated in other ways, for example statements being turned into questions through your tone of voice or the use of a question mark. But given that most questions incorporate one of these words, it's worth reflecting on the impact of different phrasing.

Why

Why questions can help us understand and get to the cause of something. They can help us question received wisdom. They encourage us to dig under the surface.

'Why do we drive on the left in the UK?' 'Why are women often paid less than men?' 'Why has it taken so long for climate change to become widely recognized as a threat?'

There is even a specific technique that can help us dig down into the root cause of a problem, called the *5 Whys*.[39] Often when we are seeking the underlying cause of an issue, the first answer that comes up is superficial and we may need to dig down more deeply. You may need to ask *why* several times, hence the name. Note that the number 5 isn't set in stone; it's an illustration of the number of times you might typically ask the question.

Here's a simple example of how 5 Whys may be helpful:

'Why am I struggling to finish this project?' Because I'm so busy.

'Why am I so busy?' Because I've taken on too many commitments.

'Why have I taken on so many commitments?' Because I underestimate how long work will take.

'Why do I underestimate how long work will take?' Because I don't log my time to get accurate data on how long tasks are taking.

'Why don't I log my time?' It hasn't really occurred to me, but it's something I can start now.

Use 'why' with caution

Although useful in many instances, *why* is also a question to be used with caution in conversations. Why? This question may be interpreted as challenging the choices that people have made, which in turn may reflect their values. The why question can therefore feel quite personal; it may result in someone feeling they need to defend their actions, values, and even their identity. And because it can provoke defensiveness, the why question can prompt people to entrench themselves further into a position. This can potentially put up barriers, rather than opening the door to mutual understanding.

'Why do you vote for xyz political party?'

'Why did you do this?'

'Why are you wearing jeans?'

So, when you need to explore causes, it can be helpful to think about your phrasing and find ways to ask exploratory questions that don't start with the word *Why*.

What, how, and what if

What and *how* questions can bring up practical solutions, making them helpful in problem solving, for example. They can also be used for root-cause analysis, and may bring up different responses to *why* questions. They are helpful in decision making and action planning.

For root-cause situations, ask questions like:

> *'How did this problem start?'*
>
> *'What happened just before the problem?'*
>
> *'What happened next?'*

For problem solving, ask questions like:

> *'How might we solve this?'*
>
> *'How do I achieve this goal?'*
>
> *'What could be the implications of doing this?'*
>
> *'What do I do first?'*

High-profile life coach Marie Forleo uses a great phrase (also the title of her book): 'Everything is figureoutable'.[40] If we want to achieve something, *how* is a question that will get us there.

Where and when

These questions point to locations in space and time. They can be helpful to drill down into the detail:

> *'Where exactly in your arm do you feel this pain?'*
>
> *'Where did you find this information?'*
>
> *'When did you first notice these symptoms?'*
>
> *'When did you speak to Sue?'*

Who and whom

Questions starting with *who* and *whom* invite the identification of individuals.

'Who would be able to help?'

'To whom should I address this reference request?'

Who questions can be helpful in avoiding generalizations:

'People won't be willing to do this.' is vague.

'Who in the team won't be willing?' seeks a more specific answer.

Clean Language

Clean Language is an approach to communication which includes a specific set of questions, designed to minimize presuppositions and assumptions. Clean Language questions allow people maximum scope to answer in their own way. It helps us to avoid the trap of thinking that other people see the world in the same way as us and instead helps us to hear, see, and appreciate how other people think.

Clean Language originates in the work of New Zealand born David Grove, a counselling psychologist, who discovered that he could help people heal from traumatic experiences by supporting them to identify and evolve their own internal representations and metaphors.[41] To do this, he found it was important to use questions that were neutral, in that they didn't introduce new ideas and metaphors, and thus influence the client's own exploration. Clean Language questions help facilitate the kind of metaphorical explorations that we looked at in Chapter 5.

Using Clean Language questions

Grove's approach and the language he used was observed and codified by James Lawley and Penny Tompkins.[42] Although originally devised within the context of therapy and coaching,

Clean Language questions are now recognized as valuable in many different contexts. They can be used in a variety of situations where you would like to gather information whilst avoiding presuppositions that could influence the results. For example, they can be used in market research, academic research, and interviews.

And Clean Language questions are valuable in building connections, personally and professionally. For example, if your child is telling you about their day, asking a few of these questions may encourage them to expand further. If a friend is telling you about their experience, this approach can help you to listen more deeply and keep your own perspective out of the picture. In problem solving at work, Clean Language questions can help you to learn more about how colleagues see a situation, avoiding the risk of jumping to conclusions too soon.

Examples of Clean Language questions

There is quite a small set of basic Clean Language questions. A key to being Clean is that you pick up accurately on some of the key words or phrases that the other person has used. You then ask a question which incorporates some of their words. Many of the questions contain xx with xx being the exact word or words that the other person has said.

Unlike some active listening approaches, you don't summarize or paraphrase in your own words. The focus is on encouraging someone to go more deeply into their own thinking, rather than checking your understanding with a summary. Instead, you build you own mental picture of the other person's world, and continually update your version of their world as you discover more about their thinking.

Here are two of the most useful and widely used questions, followed by an example of how you might use them in a conversation.

> 'What kind of [xx]?' *Or* 'What kind of [xx] is that [xx]?'

> 'Is there anything else about [xx]?'

Example:

Speaker: I would like this event to be a success.

Questioner: What kind of success is that success?

Speaker: I would like to attract a great keynote speaker.

Questioner: What kind of great keynote speaker?

Speaker: A speaker who has published a bestselling book.

Questioner: And is there anything else about that great keynote speaker?

Other commonly used Clean Language questions are:

> 'What would you like to have happen?'

> 'Then what happens? and 'What happens next?'

> 'Where is xx?'

Sequencing your questions

Using different types of questions during a conversation can help the dialogue to open up, build, deepen, and close. Questions arise naturally from listening, and it can also be helpful to consider some general principles related to the sequencing of questions. These are general principles rather than rigid rules, and you might like to observe conversations that you are participating in or observing to see what patterns you notice.

Open questions are usually the best way to start a conversation, for example: 'What's on your mind?', 'What would you like to have happen?', 'What would you like to discuss?' These avoid constraining the other person's response and give them a chance to say what they would really like to talk about.

Then as the dialogue develops, you may want to ask more probing questions to go deeper. The Clean Language questions 'what kind of…?' or a similar type of question can really help here. Pick up on what the other person is saying and allow yourself to get gently curious about what they think and feel.

Closed questions are often useful towards the end of a discussion to agree next steps. And they can be helpfully used at any stage when you wish to clarify a point or check that you've accurately understood the other person.

Safety in conversations

Questions are an important part of a conversation. They can get a conversation started and help to move it along. They can initiate a change of direction or help to restart a stalling discussion.

Used insensitively, questions can also take a discussion off track or focus on irrelevancies. They can be experienced as hostile or nosy, and they can be manipulative. In short, questions don't always facilitate connection.

A conversation can be helpfully started with questions that invite self-disclosure, but are not too exposing. For example, asking about something that happened recently allows for a wide range of replies. Small talk can help to build rapport, and can lead into a deeper conversation once a level of connection has been established.

For a conversation to reach some depth, there needs to be a sense of what is known as psychological safety. Both people need to feel that it's safe to open up and say what they really think, in the belief that they won't be ridiculed or belittled and that any criticism will be directed towards their ideas, rather than at them as a person. Building this safety can take time, particularly if the relationship is one that feels unequal, such as a manager with a member of staff that they supervise. A key to building trust and safety is to be willing to be vulnerable. Being willing to open up and share your thoughts and feelings makes it safer for other people to do so.

The role of curiosity in questioning

As we've already explored, curiosity can be a valuable attitude in building connection when it comes from a desire for insight and understanding, rather than self-gratification. Empathy can arise from being gently curious about what's important to the other person and how they see the world.

Curiosity is less helpful if your questions are more about satisfying your own desire for detail. This could be interpreted as nosiness. Before asking a probing question, it's worth asking yourself whether the question is likely to deepen the relationship or help the other person articulate their viewpoint.

Good questions arise out of a genuine interest in the other person and a desire to hear more about what they think and feel, and what matters to them. And however good your question, it may not hit the mark. It's important to be aware of how the person reacts when you ask them a question and, if necessary, ask a different question.

Practices: Noticing and playing with questions

- As you go about your day, notice what questions you're asking other people, and what kind of responses they generate.
- Reflect after a conversation: could you have phrased a question differently? What might the impact have been?
- Notice how other people use questions. If you're the one being asked a question, what impact does it have on you? If you're observing a conversation between other people, what do you notice? This doesn't have to be in person as TV interviews, or radio and podcast discussions can provide interesting examples.
- If you're completing a survey or evaluation, look at the questions you're being asked, as these will have been compiled with a particular impact in mind. Are there any presuppositions, for example? Or have the questions been designed to be as open as possible?
- Practise playing with some specific question formats, such as the Clean Language questions: 'What would you like to have happen?' 'What kind of xx?' 'Is there anything else about that xx?'

Summary: Crafting questions

- Phrase your questions carefully, being aware of the impact they can have in opening up or closing down a conversation. An awareness of sequencing can enhance, or diminish, the power of individual questions.
- To deepen your understanding of another person's perspective, Clean Language questions are helpful in avoiding presuppositions. Be careful not to use leading questions inadvertently.

- Allow yourself to be curious about how other people think and feel and how they see the world.

Your perspective?

How deliberate are you in the way you use questions and in your phrasing?

What kind of questions do you find yourself using at work?

What questions do you find particularly helpful in creating connection with others?

What changes could you make in the way you use questions?

Questions develop the shape of a conversation and are a valuable aspect of building connection between people. Understanding the impact of different types of questions, and when to use them, can help your interactions to develop in a way that enhances mutual understanding and is constructive in nature.

In the next chapter, we'll consider the role of storytelling and metaphor in creating connection and enhancing communication.

Chapter 9

Just imagine...
Story and metaphor to
engage and influence others

In this chapter we'll look at storytelling in communication, considering how to craft stories and put them to good use in communicating with others.

We'll also look at the role of metaphor in storytelling and communication, considering the power of well-chosen metaphors to engage and influence other people.

Story

Opening up a box from the attic, we came across two acrylic-bound flip photo albums, dating back to the late 1970s. My sister and I were spending time going through our late father's house. When our beloved Dad died at the age of 90, there was a lot to do, sorting out objects and photographs from his life, with decisions to be made on what to keep and what to donate.

Photographs of our family at home and on holiday acted as prompts for remembering and sharing stories from our childhood. We noticed where we had similar memories, and where we had different interpretations of the past. We reminisced and cried, and in the process the interweaving of our shared history brought us closer together. Strands of our past came together as we wove a shared blanket of memory, fibres of love, grief, and nostalgia coming together into a new understanding of who we were and who we are.

In Chapter 5, we looked briefly at how our inner narratives shape our own experience of the world. Of course, stories are also fundamental to the way we communicate with other people. We tell stories, share stories, and build stories together.

When our father died, my sister and I spent many hours going through his house, sorting out objects and photographs from his life. These acted as prompts for remembering and sharing stories from our childhood. Families, communities, companies, organizations, nations, humanity. We all have stories that bind us together, as well as stories that separate us.

Storytellers

Who tells stories? We all do. We tell stories as friends, parents, politicians, advertisers, teachers, writers, leaders. We may think of our stories as anecdotes, reports, examples, or case studies. We tell our doctors stories of our symptoms. We tell our friends stories of our family, our holidays, our experiences. We tell our children stories of our childhood. Teachers tell us stories from the worlds of history, science or literature... Advertisers tell us stories of idealized people living enviable lives. Politicians promise sunlit uplands. Leaders paint a picture of where a team or a company are heading, and why the work of an organization is important. Stories help us communicate information in a way that is visually and emotionally engaging. And within these stories, we see patterns and ideas emerging again and again.

Story structures

Story structures appear to be hardwired into the way human beings make sense of the world. This is borne out by the commonality you find in stories across cultures. Mythologists, such as Joseph Campbell and Michael Meade, have identified wisdom in ancient myths that are still relevant today. Joseph Campbell is best known for his identification of the Hero's Journey, a structure that is found in many Hollywood movies, notably *Star Wars*, and is also widely used in marketing communications.

Christopher Booker, in his book *The Seven Basic Plots*,[43] argues that a small number of narrative structures seem to underpin most storytelling, whether that's in literature, myth, or film. Here are three examples:

Rags to riches

These are tales of a child of good character, born or fallen into poverty or deprivation. Through a series of events, they are elevated to a position of wealth and enhanced status, reflective of their innate noble qualities. Examples include *Cinderella*, *Aladdin*, Eliza Doolittle in *Pygmalion*, and *Oliver Twist*.

Voyage and return

Voyage and return is a genre where the characters find themselves thrust into a sometimes fantastical world, where they experience strange and unexpected adventures, before returning to our everyday world, sometimes (although not always) altered by the experience. This genre includes children's classics like *Alice in Wonderland* and *The Lion, The Witch and The Wardrobe*. An adult example could be *Brideshead Revisited* where hero Charles Ryder experiences the world of his friend Sebastian (an ultimately tragic figure).

The quest

In this story structure, the hero is called to set out on a journey to find some form of treasure. It is a call that they cannot refuse, and in the process, they navigate a series of ordeals, such as overcoming monsters and temptations, supported by companions and helpers. After overcoming a final ordeal, the hero triumphs and gains the 'treasure'. Examples of epic quests include Homer's *Odyssey* and *The Hobbit*.

Booker's other basic plots are Overcoming the Monster, Rebirth, Comedy, and Tragedy. And he draws his analysis together by identifying a unifying factor behind all great story-telling, which is a journey from darkness into light. The hero or heroine goes through some kind of challenge or conflict which they overcome and emerge in some way altered. This book is a cracking read for anyone interested in literature, film, and the human condition. The principles can be applied to everyday stories as well as those found in literature and films. For example, we might tell the quest story on a more quotidian level, as we describe how we find our own path in life, through numerous challenges, and with the support and mentoring of others along the way.

Telling stories

When you tell a story, a starting point is to work out what you want to achieve; why do you want to tell this story? It may be:

- to get something off your chest, a problem shared…;
- to reflect on your learning from an experience;
- to help others learn through a teaching story;
- to generate a sense of belonging, for example through stories of how a business was founded;

- to demonstrate the impact of an organization, such as stories of ways that a charity has helped beneficiaries or a company has served its customers;
- to entertain;
- to gather ideas, for example, on how the story can continue or go in a different direction.

Phases of story crafting

When writing a story, it helps to think of the process as having two distinct phases.[44]

1. Distil the story down to the bones. The starting point. Key turning points in the narrative. The conclusion. The theme.
2. Then build up from this starting point by adding 'colour', creating characters, bringing the setting to life with enough detail to help the reader or listener form a picture of what is going on.

Stories are valuable in presentations, so it's no coincidence that the widely shared TED talks tend to start with a story.[45] These stories are carefully honed and rehearsed to help the speaker illustrate and share their ideas. As someone who trains and presents for a living, my stories tend to be much more informal, generally anecdotes or examples from my experience, or from books or the news, which I pull in to illustrate a point. I also love to ask people in the room for their stories and examples.

My structure

In thinking about my own stories, and in sharing ideas in workshops, I tend to use the following simple structure:

- Character
- Setting/starting point
- Problem/challenge
- Catalyst or guide for change
- Resolution – inner/outer

Here's an example from the story at the start of this chapter:

- Characters – myself and my sister
- Starting point – at my father's house after his death
- Challenge – the emotional impact of working through his effects
- Catalyst – objects prompting reflection and discussion
- Resolution – we learn more about each other through our different responses. Brings us closer together.

Stories in selling

Stories are widely used in marketing and selling. If you want to 'sell' something, even if it's an idea rather than a product or service, then stories are the secret to success.

In a marketing context, a version of the rags to riches or the quest story structure may be used by motivational speakers to show how they started with nothing and became successful, with the implication being: 'If I did it, then you can too!'

In his book *Building a StoryBrand*, Donald Miller discusses the Hero's Journey, in which the hero overcomes many obstacles before triumphing, with the help of guides and mentors along the way.[46] Miller makes the important point that ideally your customer or client should be the hero in the story, and your business or brand should be seen as the guide. It's not about you being the hero; it's about the customer achieving what they want with your help and support.

This principle holds good in situations where you're selling an idea. So, if you're a leader or manager who wants to inspire your team, make them the heroes in the story of how they can help their customers or colleagues, or achieve their goals.

Metaphor

Metaphor is integral to the way we construct our understanding of the world, as explored in Chapter 5. And metaphors are a valuable tool in bringing our ideas and stories to life, in a way that connects with others. They can turn potentially dry data into something much more tangible and relatable.

The role of metaphor in connection

Listening to other people's metaphors helps us to understand the way they see the world, and we can build on this in our storytelling and communication. As an example, I was facilitating a workshop on team leadership for a group of engineers. A delegate compared a high-performing team to an engine, with the various components all well maintained and working well. If components were neglected, then they would negatively impact the overall performance of the engine. This metaphor worked well for a group of engineers. But in thinking about how to potentially influence colleagues who weren't engineers, it might be helpful to look at adapting the metaphor. As someone who has trained in drama, I see a high-performing team as an ensemble production. Everyone plays a variety of roles and it's not about individual star performers; instead, it's about working in harmony to create something of value.

From a wider perspective, metaphors in common use are shaped by the times, and then in turn shape how we see the world. For example, in the 16th and 17th centuries, ideas emerged of man as machine.[47] Thinking of people as composed of parts has allowed for specialisms in medicine, for example, but in the process the holistic and interrelated nature of a person is at risk of being overlooked.

In recent years it's become commonplace to use the metaphor of the brain being a computer. We talk of hacking our brains. Programmers for social media platforms such as Facebook allegedly use algorithms to deliberately try and stimulate the production of neurotransmitters in our brains to influence our behaviours.[48]

Listening to someone's habitual metaphorical language will give you an insight into how they see the world and provide a framework for connection. If someone uses a lot of construction metaphors, how can you build on these? If someone uses numerous natural metaphors, how can you grow your relationship and allow it to blossom? If someone uses sporting metaphor, how you can ensure you're on the same team?

Not everyone will respond positively to metaphorical language.[49] So as with any communication, maintain an awareness of how the other person is reacting, and be prepared to be flexible in your approach.

Packaging your perspective

Storytelling and metaphor are vehicles for conveying thoughts and ideas; in taking what is in our experience and thinking, and packaging it in a way that makes sense to others. In words attributed to Jean-Luc Godard: 'Sometimes reality is too complex. Stories give it form'.[50] Finding the right story structure or metaphor will help you bridge the gap between your mind and message, and the minds of other people.

Practices

Storytelling

Try breaking down a story from your experience, think about:

- What are the bullet points of the story: starting points; key turning points or changes in the narrative; resolution?
- What is the overarching plot structure?
- What detail will help to bring the story to life without overdoing it?
- When telling the story, where will be your starting point? This isn't necessarily the beginning; you might start with a turning point, for example, and then return to the starting point.

Metaphor

- In conversation, listen out for metaphors that other people use. Are there patterns in how a person is describing their experience?
- What metaphors can you use to liven up your communication?

Summary: Crafting story

- We all use story to structure and communicate with other people.
- There is a set of basic structures that underpin satisfying stories, and these can be applied to different communication contexts.
- Metaphors reflect the thinking of the era we live in, as well as individuals' contexts and thought processes.

- We can enhance communication by noticing and building on other people's metaphorical representations.

 Your perspective?

Are there any story structures that you use repeatedly in the way you communicate?

How might you tell a version of your career or life story, casting yourself as the hero/heroine?

How might you describe your profession or business, casting your customers or clients as the heroes?

What metaphors would you use to describe your team or workplace culture?

How aware are you of the language, stories, and metaphors that other people use in conversation?

 Story and metaphor can enhance connection by bringing structure, relevance, and emotional impact to your communication.

As much as words are important in communication, they are only part of the story. In the next chapter we consider the important role that our bodies and voices have in building connection with others.

Chapter 10

It's more than words
Body and voice in the dance
of connection

Connection involves much more than the words we use to communicate. Our tone of voice and body language helps to elevate face-to-face interactions from those of the written word. Bringing ourselves more deeply into connection with our whole-body intelligence can also enhance and elevate our relationships with others.

We naturally mirror other people, and the use of empathic body language helps to create rapport. Expanding our physical and vocal awareness can also help us communicate more authentically and with more vitality.

This integration of words, movement and voice isn't about learning 'tricks' of body language (although these can be helpful in certain situations such as public speaking). It's more about feeling into your body so that you stay connected with your own physical being as you communicate with others. It's the ability to centre yourself quickly when you're metaphorically knocked off balance. And it's about building up your physical presence and vocal range so they can more accurately express what's inside.

In this chapter, we'll look at the role of body language, including facial expressions and the use of gestures. And we'll consider ways to develop our voices to communicate in a way that is both authentic and impactful.

The dance of connection

Partner dancing requires connection at all three levels: with yourself, with your dance partner, and within the social context, which will include the music and the presence of other dancers.

To draw an analogy with any kind of communication, you first need to build that connection with yourself. You need to be able to maintain some level of awareness of your own reactions as you build the knowledge of the 'dance steps', the practical communication skills needed to connect.

You also need to be aware of the other person, your meta-phorical dance partner, and to allow them to affect you. In a conversation you will sometimes take the lead and other times be responding. A great conversation is co-created between two or more people, and it can generate understanding and insights that you couldn't have created alone.

And like a dance, a conversation takes place in a wider context. This includes your history, the other person's history, the culture within which you reside, the relationship that you already have between you, and the direction in which the relationship is heading.

Tuning in to your partner

Connecting with others involves three aspects: the words you use, your voice, your physical expression which includes your facial expressions, and body language such as your posture and gestures.

I would like to say a word here about the relative importance of these three aspects. There is a much-misquoted piece of research undertaken by Albert Mehrabian which is often inter-preted as demonstrating that only 7% of communication is conveyed by your words.[51] This isn't universally applicable, yet you'll still hear many people using this statistic as if it's a fact. I remember attending a mentoring course some years ago where we were required to answer an assessment at the end, and one of the questions required you to know this 'fact'. No wonder the 7% figure has become so widely used.

Instead, what the research does show is that if there is a mismatch between your words, and your physical and vocal communication, the latter two can have significantly more impact than the former. So, for powerful and effective communication, there needs to be congruence between all three aspects: words, body language, and tone of voice.

This is easy to picture if you imagine an exaggerated example. A colleague may be saying that she's happy to take on a new piece of work. However, you see her face is furrowed, her fists are clenched, and her tone of voice conveys irritation. What do you infer about her real feelings?

Observe rather than judge

In real life, the effect is often less exaggerated, but you will still pick up important messages from someone's non-verbal communication. And the dance of connection is about tuning in to other people's body language and facial expressions. This means noticing changes in other people, as a witness or observer, rather than making assumptions about what this means. Crossed arms may not necessarily mean someone is defensive. If someone's looking away that may not mean they are shy. If you interpret and label someone's body language, you are judging them. And judgement hinders connection.

Instead of making snap judgements, use your observations to perhaps prompt a question or to remind you to check your own body language – could they be mirroring what you're doing?

Your face tells a story

When it comes to facial expression, there is an interesting fact that although we have a certain amount of control over our facial expressions, our initial emotional expressions in response to a stimulus may not come from our conscious mind. Paul Eckman[52] and others have undertaken research into what are referred to as micro-expressions.[53] These are involuntary emotional responses triggered by the amygdala, reflecting what are considered the seven universal human emotions: anger, contempt, disgust, fear, happiness, sadness, and surprise. These micro-expressions last a tiny fraction of a second and may not be consciously registered. By being more present and aware of others' reactions, we can pick up more accurately on emotional reactions and build our empathy and sense of connection.

Having said that, because our initial instinctive responses are evolved to protect us from harm, these initial reactions may be tempered by our logical mind. For example, if we hear a fact that we were not expecting, we may initially feel surprise or fear, but quickly realize that this isn't truly a threat. Our initial emotional responses are truthful in the moment, but may be modified, and the modification may not necessarily be untrue. Empathic connection seeks to understand, not to judge or prematurely assess.

In harmony – the role of rapport

One Sunday morning, I settled down in the elegant sitting room of a flat in Swiss Cottage in London. It was the second day of a training course in NLP (Neuro Linguistic Programming), and our small group were gathered to learn about rapport. Rapport is a term used to describe a relationship in which the people concerned are 'in sync' with each other and communicate in a smooth and harmonious way. Our teacher apologized for having woken up with a cold which had, overnight, brought on a low and husky voice.

She shared ideas from NLP about rapport, suggesting that in order to build rapport and good communication, it could be helpful to deliberately 'match' the other person's style, including their physicality and tone of voice. I asked a question and suddenly noticed that, without consciously doing so, I had dropped my voice to a much lower tone, more closely matched to our teacher.

In general, I'm not a fan of deliberately matching your voice or body to simulate rapport. This is because I believe the best way to achieve connection is to listen with attention, curiosity, and a non-judgemental attitude. Rapport builds naturally through the process of empathic listening. You can in theory fake this through deliberate adjustment, but a risk is that if you don't do this with skill, it may be obvious, and the other person could interpret your efforts negatively. I also believe that if you're spending all your time focusing on trying to look as if you're in rapport, you're not spending the time listening actively!

Having said that, this technique can be helpful if used sparingly. If you're in a conversation and notice that you're on a very different wavelength to another person, it can be helpful to make small adjustments. For example, if you naturally speak quickly and your partner speaks more slowly, you might choose just to slow down a little. And if you notice that you are leaning forward and making a lot of physical gestures, yet your partner is sitting back, you might shift your posture back a little and give them more space.

The value here is in awareness and adjustment, as you would adjust to the tempo of your dance partner.

And if you are mirroring each other, is this in a positive way? If you notice some tension or discomfort in your body, it is quite likely that the other person is also experiencing this. If you can relax and release tension in your own physicality, this can be picked up by the other person and potentially help them relax. Thus, you can influence and lead someone subtly through skilful attention to your own body language and sensations, and awareness of the impact these have on others.

Are there people with whom you feel relaxed and comfortable? Can you identify something about the way they hold themselves that is helpful to you?

Using gesture

As someone who talks a lot with my hands, I'm aware of both the benefits and pitfalls of this mode of communication. It can bring words to life. I sometimes observe myself and my hands are naturally making representations of what I am seeing in the space around me. This may be helpful to people who are trying to understand my points. If you are someone who uses gesture naturally, you may find this gives a more three-dimensional aspect to your communication than words alone.

Gesture can also be used deliberately in formal communication situations such as presentations. A tip here is to remember that if you gesture from right to left, your audience will read this from left to right. If, for example, you're gesturing to show a graph or bell curve, you might want to reverse what you're seeing. I try to remember to do this in formal presentations, or where it could really help the other person's understanding of a concept by making it come more visually alive in space.

But be aware that there can be drawbacks to over-use of gesture, particularly when you're listening to other people. It may be distracting, for example. When I trained as a Clean Language Facilitator, the hardest part of the work for me was unlearning my natural use of gesture. I gradually became more skilled at noticing my own gestures and now try to use them less when I'm in listening mode unless there's a specific reason, such as gesturing to a point in space where the other person has directed their attention as a way of reflecting what I'm seeing and hearing.

The role of your voice

Aside from words and body language, voice is the other component of spoken communication. And our voices are important for connection.

Think about how you feel when you hear the voice of a loved one, or the voice of a trusted colleague, or the voice of someone who tends to set your teeth on edge. Think about how a skilled actor or singer can make you feel with their voice, even if you set aside the words they say. Your unique voice is influenced by external factors such as the accents you heard whilst growing up and by your physicality; hence female voices are typically higher pitched than male voices.

There are three components to voice production: breath, resonance, and articulation. All these can be developed to give your voice a better sound quality. In developing your voice, it's not about trying to change your voice so that it's not authentically yours. Instead, it's about developing your innate vocal capacity, so your voice is the best that it can naturally be.

Sound is made when your breath travels over your vocal cords as you speak. Learning to breathe deeply, from your diaphragm, will help to give more power to your voice.

The sound resonates in the chambers of your body, including your mouth and your chest. Exercises to improve resonance will give your voice more richness, depth, and variety.

Words are articulated by the movements of your mouth, lips, and tongue. Physically exercising these muscles will help you articulate more clearly. Exercises can also help overcome minor speech impediments; for example, I used to pronounce the letter **r** as being closer to **w**. I have largely eliminated this using an exercise learnt from James Dodding, a wonderful voice teacher with whom I was fortunate enough to take classes at the City Lit in London.

Learning how to develop my voice has been a hugely valuable and empowering experience for me. It underpins much of my current work where I speak, facilitate, and train others. I've gone from being a somewhat timid and quiet speaker to someone who can now comfortably fill a decent-sized room with my voice. And I always go through some vocal exercises and warmups in preparation for any substantial speaking appointment.

There are some great voice books available, often written by voice coaches with experience of working with actors and other professional speakers. The book that I most often recommend to clients is Patsy Rodenburg's *The Right to Speak*.[54]

Using your voice

Here are some tips for speaking with impact, such as when you want to connect with others with the aim of influencing or inspiring them to action. And you'll find some simple exercises for developing aspects of voice production later in this chapter.

If you have a difficult message to share, practise speaking key phrases out loud, so that saying them starts to feel natural. If you lack confidence in what you are saying, or feel uncomfortable or awkward, this can make it more difficult for the listener too. Being able to bring the qualities of both empathy and clarity will help you to tackle difficult conversations.

If you want your statements to sound authoritative and have impact, check that when you're stating something it doesn't come over as tentative or a question. This can happen if your voice rises at the end of a sentence. If you want to sound more authoritative, allow your voice to deepen slightly at the end of a sentence, which conveys a sense of gravitas. This may help you to be taken more seriously and potentially have a positive impact on your career, particularly if you are in a leadership role or aspire to be a leader.

To develop your voice, it can be helpful to record yourself speaking and listen back.

Remember that your voice sounds different in real life than from a recording on your phone or computer. If you don't like the sound of your voice, remember that you almost certainly sound better in person. But listening to a recording will give you pointers for areas to improve upon. And if you record yourself a few weeks later, after doing regular voice exercises, you may be pleasantly surprised by the difference.

The 'music'

Non-verbal communication takes place within a wider societal and cultural context. I am a neurotypical white woman who has lived my life in the UK and Europe, and my experience is set in this context. Although I've been fortunate to work with some diverse groups within the UK, I'm not an expert in cross-cultural communication. So, all I want to do here is briefly highlight some areas of communication where you may experience difference. If you work or communicate extensively across cultures, it's worth getting some specialist training or reading more on the subject.

Distance/personal boundaries

We all have our boundaries in terms of how close we stand to other people, depending on how well we know them. These are both cultural and personal. You've probably had the occasional experience of someone standing 'too close', and yet this doesn't happen very often. Even in crowded places such as an underground train, people give each other space and only gradually get closer as a train fills up. Some people are less comfortable with proximity than others of course, and some people find it harder to learn these unspoken 'rules'. But when you're mixing with people from different cultures, you may find people naturally stand closer or further away, depending on how reserved the culture is.

Gestures

Gestures can mean different things in different countries, and there is a risk of being unintentionally insulting; for example, in some countries a thumbs-up sign is akin to a much ruder hand gesture. And nodding, for example, isn't a universal sign for 'yes'; in Bulgaria it means 'no'.

Eye contact

Eye contact varies by culture. The relaxed eye contact that I have suggested in earlier chapters is appropriate in the UK cultural context but may not be so everywhere. In some Middle Eastern cultures, people may hold more sustained eye contact with people of the same gender, but only brief eye contact with people of the opposite sex.

Observation is key

Aside from researching specific cultural norms, observation is your friend. Noticing how people behave will allow you to adapt your behaviour. And be aware of your own comfort zone too. Being willing and able to adapt is a positive trait, but not to the extent that you lose connection with yourself and your own needs. If you require more personal space for example, you may need to politely and respectfully express this and explain why.

Practices: Developing your voice

Breathing from the diaphragm

A strong voice comes from diaphragmatic breathing – where your breath comes from deep in your lungs, pushed out by your diaphragm, rather than from high up in your chest.

To feel this, sit up straight or stand, then rest your hands on your lower ribs.

Breathe out as much air as you can, pulling in your stomach so that the lungs empty, and feel this under your hands.

Then relax and feel your stomach pushing out; this creates a vacuum in the lower part of the lungs and pulls in fresh air.

When we get nervous, we often breathe in a shallow way. Breathing from your belly will give your voice much more power.

Sensible warning – if at any time you feel dizzy when practising breathing exercises, then stop and breathe normally.

Some forms of exercises like yoga and Pilates will help you develop your ability to breathe deeply.

Resonance

Sound resonates in chambers of the body such as the chest, throat, mouth, and sinuses. Imagine your body as a musical instrument. If you play a violin, for example, the tone is produced as the sounds from the bow crossing the string resonate in the body and materials that make up the instrument.

A simple way to warm up your voice and improve resonance is to hum. Make a 'mmmmm' sound with your mouth lightly closed. Feel the resonance in your mouth. Imagine the resonance moving down your throat and into your chest. And then imagine it moving up and around inside your head.

Articulation

Clear articulation is helped by exercises to strengthen the muscles in and around your mouth, including your lips and tongue. For articulation, practise a few tongue twisters.

Peter Piper picked a peck of pickled pepper will exercise the lips.

Two toads totally tired of trying to trot to Tetbury will provide a workout for the tip of the tongue.

Gobbling gargoyles gobbled gobbling goblins will exercise the back of the tongue.

Vocal variety

A good voice is varied rather than monotonous. If your voice lacks variety, then an exercise to improve this aspect is to practise exaggerating the way you speak. You can do this on your own; just pick up a book or magazine and read the words with what seems like much too much expression. Ham it up! This will help you develop more vocal variety. Try recording your exaggerated version. It may in fact sound just right. Or you may need to tone it down a little in real life, once you've developed the ability to speak with more variety. You can do this on your own of course or, even better, practise with another person. Have fun with it!

Practice: Body posture

Look at your posture. Ideally you will be upright but not rigid. Allow your head to float gently upwards. Imagine a golden thread connecting the crown of your head with the heavens. Relax your shoulders. Feel your feet firmly connected to the floor.

Before you go into a meeting (in private), give your hands and arms a shake; even shake your whole body if you have a space where you can do this privately and safely. Consciously decide to let go of any worries or distractions and that you're shaking them out and letting them go.

Summary: Crafting the dance of connection

- Where your words don't match your body language and voice, the latter may have more impact.
- Be aware of your posture; allow yourself to be both upright and relaxed.
- Use gestures to support communication, whilst being aware of cultural differences where relevant.
- Add depth and expression to your voice using a variety of pitch and tone and clear articulation.

Your perspective?

How much awareness do you give to your own posture and use of gesture in communication?

To what extent do you make assumptions about what other people think, based on their non-verbal communication?

To what extent does your vocal delivery affect your impact at work?

What, if anything, might you like to do to develop your voice?

In this chapter, you've explored the role of your body language and voice in building connection with other people whilst expressing yourself clearly. In the dance of connection, maintaining awareness of yourself and the other person will help you to build rapport, and enhance communication, in a way that words alone can't do.

In the next chapter we'll focus in on a specific skill that can enhance connection when it's done well. Giving and receiving quality feedback allows for honest and open communication, and it supports personal and professional development.

Chapter 11

Another perspective
Giving and receiving
feedback

According to the Collins Dictionary: 'if you get feedback on your work or progress, someone tells you how well or badly you are doing, and how you could improve. If you get good feedback you have worked or performed well'.[55]

Feedback matters because it provides a perspective that we can't possibly take ourselves: the point of view of someone who sees us from the outside. Without some honest external input, we can, and do, fool ourselves. We can be blind to some of our strengths and successes, as well as sometimes not realizing that there is still room for improvement.

As the Collins definition suggests, the term feedback is often used in a professional context where we receive helpful information about our performance, measured against our workplace objectives. Or, at least, we should receive helpful feedback. In my years of developing team leaders and teams, I've heard many people in the workplace admit they could improve how they give feedback. The tips in this chapter are based primarily on training programmes that I've facilitated in the context of working relationships. But feedback is valuable in all areas of our lives, not just at work.

Feedback offers us the gift of another person's perspective, based on what they observe and how they experience us. And of course, we can give this gift to others through our feedback. My husband is known for being very frank in his feedback and, although not always comfortable, I appreciate that I can ask him for his view and receive an honest answer, offered with a helpful intention. However, feedback does need to be given with care. Some people are very sensitive to perceived criticism and it's important to think carefully about whether, when, and how to offer feedback to others.

When given with honesty, and with consideration and respect for the other person, feedback can help build connection with others. By connecting within, we can make a wise decision as to whether we need to offer feedback at all. For example, if we find ourselves over-reacting to a small mistake, we may need to deal primarily with managing our own reactions to someone's behaviour. And connecting within can help us assess whether it would be beneficial to speak out, for example where we have positive comments to make, or where we believe our perspective may be helpful to the other person's professional or personal development. Giving thoughtful feedback allows us to be genuine with others, which can help us to build honest and valuable relationships.

In this chapter we'll look at the impact and benefits of feedback, and consider how to give different kinds of feedback, and how to receive and respond to feedback from others.

Johari Window

The Johari Window was developed by Joseph Luft and Harrington Ingham in 1955.[56]

The model is based on two axes. The first axis considers what is known or not known to self. This refers to aspects of our behaviour of which we are currently aware, or not yet aware.

The second axis is around what is known or not known to others. What can people observe or infer from our behaviour (including our words, voice and body language, actions etc.)?

The two axes give rise to four areas, described below. This model provides a framework for understanding how both feedback and self-disclosure are helpful for self-development, and for developing a more authentic connection with others. The aim is to increase the *open area*, where we show up as how we truly are. In my interpretation of the model shown below, I've included summary phrases to represent the different areas.

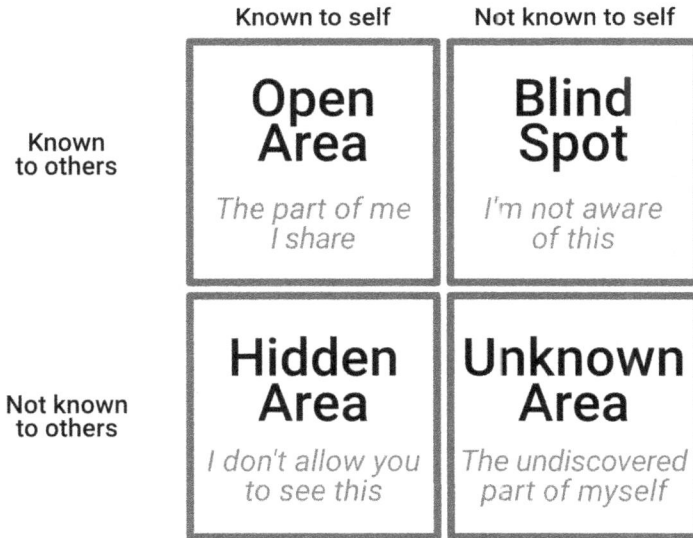

	Known to self	Not known to self
Known to others	**Open Area** *The part of me I share*	**Blind Spot** *I'm not aware of this*
Not known to others	**Hidden Area** *I don't allow you to see this*	**Unknown Area** *The undiscovered part of myself*

'The part of me I share'

Known as the *open area*, this includes those aspects of yourself that you're aware of, and that you're willing to show to others. Essentially, the more of yourself that you're willing to disclose, the bigger your open area. The open area includes both your strengths and positive attributes, and your vulnerabilities and weaknesses. When someone gets to know you well, the open area between you expands, and the other person sees more of your humanity – your brilliance and your shadows.

'I don't allow you to see this'

Known as the *hidden area*, this includes parts of you of which you are aware but that you choose not to disclose to others. These may include parts of yourself that feel emotionally tender or vulnerable, as well as parts of yourself that don't fit the positive self-image that you may like to project. Maybe you are more competitive, or judgemental, or uncertain than you'd like to admit.

To increase your willingness to be more open, it can be helpful to understand and accept yourself more deeply and compassionately – a key theme of this book. And then you need to be willing to share your inner world with others and not to be afraid of being seen.

A benefit of sharing more of yourself is that your open area expands, allowing people to get to know you more deeply. And your increased openness can make it easier for other people to open up too, thus making space for a more truthful and authentic connection.

'I'm not aware of this'

Known as your *blind spot*, this area contains aspects of your behaviour, body language, and personality that other people can see, but of which you are unaware.

The blind spot normally includes positive aspects of your being. You can see your intention but not necessarily the impact of what you say and do. And it may also include some behaviours which have a negative impact on other people, of which you are unaware.

Feedback opens the door to enhanced self-knowledge. Feedback can help you to reduce the size of your blind spot, and thus expand your open area.

'The undiscovered part of myself'

This *unknown area* covers those parts of your psyche which are currently unknown to both yourself and others. These may be patterns within your subconscious mind that may only emerge in certain circumstances. This may include hidden talents and strengths. It may also include vulnerabilities.

Self-development activities allow you to gradually bring aspects of the unknown into your awareness. As does life. As we experience more, we learn more about ourselves. A key to uncovering the unknown is reflective practice.[57] Reflecting on our experiences after the event helps us to make sense of our actions, draw out learning, and spot patterns of reaction and behaviour in ourselves.

Giving feedback

You should only offer feedback with the intention of providing useful information to help another person. Given with skill, feedback can be encouraging and motivating, as well as helping people identify blind spots.

Given poorly, feedback can alienate the person on the receiving end. They may end up feeling defensive or knocked back. This reduces the likelihood that they will get value from your feedback, and it can potentially be damaging to the relationship.

Don't shy away from offering feedback. But do take the time to think carefully about what you're going to say and how you're going to say it.

Giving feedback is essentially giving your perspective on another person's behaviour and the impact of the behaviour. I would recommend that you focus most of your efforts on taking the time to give people positive feedback to acknowledge that they've done something well or been helpful to you or other people.

Sometimes you may want or need to offer feedback on less helpful aspects of a person's behaviour. Take a moment to work out why you are doing this. Is it to offload your own irritation, for example (clearly not a good reason!)? Or is it in service of a more open and honest relationship, and to help the other person develop their understanding and reduce their blind spots? Feedback that is intended to encourage learning and improvement is called constructive or developmental feedback.

The value and impact of positive feedback

Have you ever found yourself assuming that feedback is only about being constructive and offering or receiving suggestions for improvement? Yes, that can be part of it. But I would argue that wholly positive feedback can be even more valuable.

Positive feedback helps to reinforce positive behaviour. If you do something well, and it's noticed and appreciated, how does that make you feel? Would you be more inclined to do more of what's working?

Positive feedback is very affirming. Most of us like to be acknowledged and appreciated, and positive feedback is a way of showing that we have noticed another person's efforts, skills, and achievements.

Positive feedback can help other people to learn and develop. To give you a work-based example: imagine you work with a colleague who normally submits reports that are informative but over-wordy and difficult to wade through. Then one week she is more concise and her report is structured with a summary of key points. If you notice and let her know that you found the revised format helpful, she is more likely to continue doing this in future.

Or a domestic example: if your partner or flatmate makes a particularly nice meal, let them know what you enjoyed most about it.

I would suggest that most of your feedback is positive in nature. This doesn't mean that you should shy away from giving constructive or critical feedback when it's called for. But noticing and appreciating the positive provides a great baseline for feedback. As well as being motivating and developmental, regular positive feedback helps to create an environment or culture where people welcome this input. When people feel their efforts are noticed and appreciated by team members, this encourages people to work hard and perform well. It creates a better atmosphere in the team. If you're a leader or manager, be a role model in giving positive feedback when you can. And encourage people to give each other positive feedback, for example by making time for this in team meetings. And if you're not in a leadership role, try taking the initiative and giving co-workers positive feedback and appreciation of their efforts.

Principles for giving constructive or critical feedback

In situations where you need to give constructive, or even critical feedback, take time to think about how to phrase your feedback and what the impact on the other person may be. You may choose to invite the other person to self-assess first: 'how do you think that went?', as they may already have identified problems and areas for improvement. If they are unaware of the need for change, then you can offer another perspective.

Feedback should be based on specific observable behaviour or verifiable information rather than your interpretation of others' behaviour. The iceberg model is helpful as a way of showing where to focus your feedback.

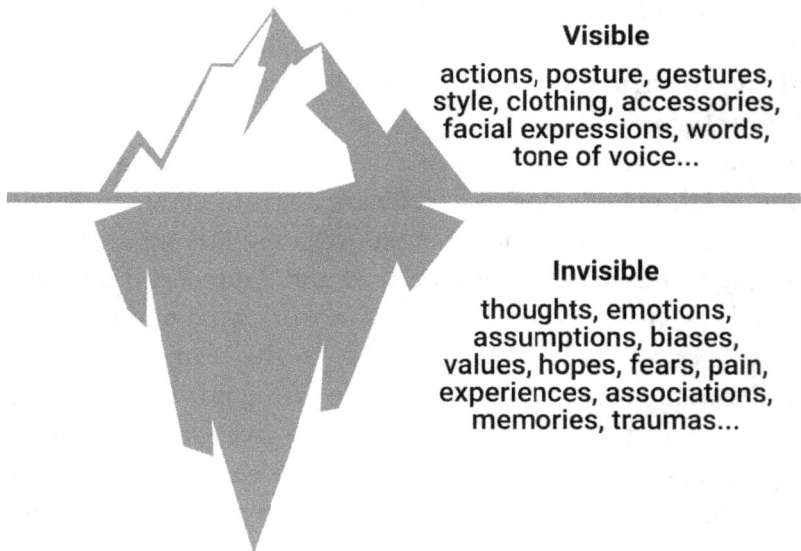

Visible
actions, posture, gestures, style, clothing, accessories, facial expressions, words, tone of voice...

Invisible
thoughts, emotions, assumptions, biases, values, hopes, fears, pain, experiences, associations, memories, traumas...

The iceberg represents the human being, and in this metaphor the part of the iceberg above the waterline represents the aspects of ourselves that others can observe. This includes our words, tone of voice, facial expressions, body language, and actions.

And as with a physical iceberg, most of our psyche is metaphorically hidden under the waterline. This includes our thoughts, fears, emotions, previous experiences, biases, assumptions, values, physical discomfort etc. Some of these elements can be inferred from our behaviour above the waterline. But we can't know for certain what lies underneath someone's behaviour unless they tell us.

So when you're offering feedback, confine your observations to what is above the waterline. And then open up a conversation, if necessary, to bring out and explore what may lie underneath.

Describe what you have noticed, the specific words and actions. Explain the effect or impact of the behaviour, for example this might be the perspective of another person who has been on the receiving end. It can be helpful to use 'I' statements when describing behaviour that affected you directly, for example 'When you arrived half an hour after our agreed time, this meant I was unable to pick my daughter up at the end of the school day' rather than 'you let me down'. The latter tends to judgemental or accusatory. If you want to express your feelings, then own the feelings: 'I felt upset that my daughter would be worried and the school inconvenienced'.

When and where to give feedback

Don't give too much feedback at once as this could be overwhelming. And do give feedback in a timely manner, as soon as possible after the event. Leaving it too long may mean the other person has forgotten what happened. And it can allow for negative feelings to build up so that you end up being less calm and measured than you would like. Having said that, if you do feel angry, it may be better to wait until you have calmed down before giving feedback, without leaving it too long. There's a balance to be struck here.

And do make sure you choose an appropriate setting. This is likely to be in private for sensitive or negative feedback, but may be a public setting for some positive feedback. Some feedback is worth giving in writing, where it can be revisited and reviewed. Personally I love receiving positive feedback in writing, so I can re-read it.

Constructive feedback is sometimes best given in writing, so you can review and digest what needs to be done next. But where you have potentially difficult feedback, it is often better to give this via a conversation, so that you check that your observations have been heard and understood. And it gives you the potential to start a conversation about what may be below the waterline. For example, you may have observed work handed in late; the other person may have been dealing with a personal issue or competing priorities and have done everything they could to complete the work. Verbal feedback can then be followed up in writing, where necessary.

The AIDA model

This simple model can be used for both positive and constructive feedback. AIDA stands for Action, Impact, Do, Accountability.

Action – what specific actions, words, or behaviours did you observe?

Impact – what was the impact or result of the actions, words or behaviours?

Do – what could you do differently or keep on doing?

Accountability – how will you ensure actions are completed? Will it help to set yourself a deadline? Do you need to check in with your manager or a coach?

For positive feedback, you may only want to cover the action and impact, followed by a simple and sincere 'thank you'.

Receiving and responding to feedback

Feedback can be seen as gift. Someone has taken the trouble to give us their perspective, and this can help us to learn and grow. But remember that one person's feedback is just one person's viewpoint. If you receive a piece of feedback that surprises or shocks you, remember that it isn't necessarily true, or the whole truth. It might however be a prompt to ask for more feedback from other people.

Just as it's important to give feedback that's objective, it's important to be aware of how feedback is given to you. Imagine that someone gives you a piece of non-objective judgemental feedback such as: 'you're selfish'. It would be easy to react defensively and say something like: 'No I'm not'. Instead, try and stay calm and ask for more objective information. 'I hear that you think I've been selfish, please can you let me know what's behind those words? What specifically could I do differently?' This may not always be easy to do; however, this kind of response can create a conversation and give you more insight into that person's viewpoint.

Once you've heard and understood the feedback, I've found it helpful to say thank you and say that you'll give it some thought. If on reflection you think the feedback was unfair, then say so, but it's often better to do this with the benefit of some thinking time. If the feedback is factually inaccurate, then of course correct this as soon as you can. The other person may simply not be aware of all the relevant facts.

With positive feedback, do also take time to reflect on what has been said. Some people find it easier to receive positive feedback than others, so if you find it difficult, reflect on this too. Is there a pattern in your resistance to positive feedback or praise? Where could this reaction have come from? What happens if you allow yourself to really hear, and take on board, positive comments?

⟲O⟳ Practices

Give more positive feedback

Practise giving more positive feedback and appreciation to people in your life. Go beyond a general 'thank you' or 'well done'. Pick out something specific that you like or appreciate.

Seek out feedback

Proactively seek more feedback from others. Ask 'What do you think? What went well? What could I do differently or better next time?'. Accept the feedback with grace and reflect on anything that surprised you. We can learn both from feedback and from our reactions to feedback.

Use reflective practice for self-awareness

Proactively use reflective practice to understand yourself better. I find writing in a journal, ideally by hand, helps to deepen self-understanding. My preference is a spiral-bound journal. This helps free me up to write honestly and openly, knowing that I can tear out the page if it feels too vulnerable, without damaging the book. I rarely tear out a page, but it does make the process of writing feel very safe, and I can express thoughts that I wouldn't be comfortable sharing out loud.

For me, I find writing brings new ideas and understandings to the surface. And it often leads me into a quieter state of mind as I safely capture my swirling thoughts on the page.

Summary: Crafting feedback

- In giving feedback, be specific, and be careful to differentiate between facts and interpretations.
- Give plenty of positive feedback.
- Be open to receiving feedback. It can provide valuable information to help you overcome blind spots and expand your levels of self-awareness.
- Remember, one person's feedback is just one person's perspective. If you are struggling to see the validity, ask more questions of that person. And seek additional feedback from others to help you identify whether there are recurring patterns in how other people experience your behaviour.
- Reflective practice can help you understand more about your unconscious thoughts and feelings and increase self-knowledge.

Your perspective?

What is your immediate reaction to the idea of receiving feedback?

What kind of feedback do you receive at work?

How easy do you find it to give feedback?

Are there instances where you could give more positive feedback to others?

In this chapter you've considered the value of giving and receiving positive and constructive feedback. You've looked at how receiving feedback can help you to overcome blind spots and understand yourself more clearly, and at how giving honest and thoughtful feedback and appreciation can help you to relate more openly with others, whether that's through offering appreciation or constructive comments.

We'll now move on to a section focused on the networks and communities of which we are a part. We're all embedded socially and professionally in a web of interconnections. Paying conscious attention to these can enhance our career and business prospects, as well as our social lives and our ability to make a meaningful contribution to the wellbeing of others. The next chapter looks at the breadth and depth of our existing networks.

Dimension 3

Connecting Beyond

We are each linked to numerous other people, organizations, communities, and social structures. Connection beyond our immediate circle keeps us participating and engaging in society. It's important for our wellbeing, both material and psychological.

I'm not primarily talking here about social media, the online web of platform-mediated relationships that link us. Social media does have a valuable role to play in enabling us to meet people with interests in common. And the strength of social media, in my view, is the way it can help us to stay in touch and maintain ongoing relationships with others. But it can also lead to feelings of exclusion and disconnection as we compare our inner worlds, with all their light and shadow, with the often sanitized and occasionally sickening words and images that can assail us online. And trying to keep up with too many people online can be a distraction from the deeper relationships that may be right in front of our faces.

Relationships emerge from conversations that can build, mend or destroy bridges, and community emerges from a network of relationships and common experiences or interests. Understanding our own network and linked relationships can help us develop and grow our sense of being integrated into the wider community. And where we see gaps in our connections, we can find ways to fill them.

In this section, I invite you to consider the dimension of connecting beyond your immediate circle of friends, family, and colleagues. What networks and communities are you part of? How do you contribute to, and benefit from, the web of social connections that bind us together? What is missing in your existing network?

And we'll end this section by taking an expanded perspective. We'll consider the value of connecting beyond ourselves, in helping us bring meaning to our individual lives by putting them in a context and acknowledging both our uniqueness and interconnection. Our understanding of the world emerges as our personal history, psychology and physiology meet and respond to external reality.

Our web of interconnection is never static; we ourselves are constantly changing, as is everything around us. Our relationships, our networks, our connections, our community, and the fabric of the material world is always shifting and changing, and there is value in becoming increasingly aware and appreciative of the wider interconnections that affect our lives.

My hope is that this section will give you some practical ideas for networking and creating community, along with some takeaway food for thought.

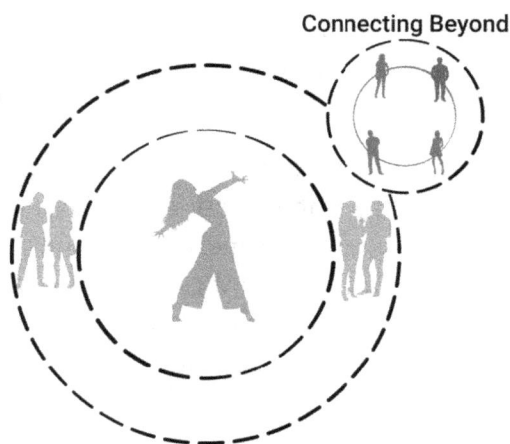

Connecting Beyond

Chapter 12

Finding community Engaging with deep and shallow networks

Connection begins with understanding yourself and being open to understanding another person. Beyond our close relationships, we are all integrated into networks and communities that intertwine and make up the social fabric of our lives. Taking some time to think about your networks and communities can help you identify connections that are truly valuable and worthwhile, and those which are less so. It can also help you to think about any gaps that you could fill, whether that's by finding new networks and communities, or even starting your own.

In this chapter we'll consider different types of networks. We'll also look at how to map your existing network, and questions to ask yourself when it comes to extending or deepening your professional and social connections.

Deep and shallow networks

One definition of a network is 'a usually informally interconnected group or association of persons (such as friends or professional colleagues)'.[58] Within your professional, friendship, and interest-group networks, you'll find different levels of closeness and interconnection.

Deep networks consist of those people you know well. These are the people that you are happy to contact if you need support or advice. You know them well enough to be willing and able to help them, and that you're happy to be associated with them. These are people with whom you have built a level of trust and mutual understanding, people to whom you have strong ties.

Shallow networks are more extensive. Your extended network may include people you've met occasionally; people that you perhaps only stay in touch with via social media; people you've known in the past but aren't currently actively in contact with. It may include people who are part of your wider community but aren't well known to you personally. For example, fellow members of a professional association who you could potentially get to know in future. These are sometimes referred to as your weak ties.[59]

Your shallow network extends to second and third-degree connections – people who know people whom you know, and the people who know them. There is evidence that we can influence, and be influenced, as far out as our third-degree connections.[60] Even our levels of happiness can, to some extent, influence the happiness of friends of friends of our friends. And vice versa. The figure below illustrates how those third-degree connections are still potentially able to influence us and be influenced by us, although to a lesser degree than our direct connections, in the darker inner circles. And we have a route to reach these people, through our direct connections and those they know.

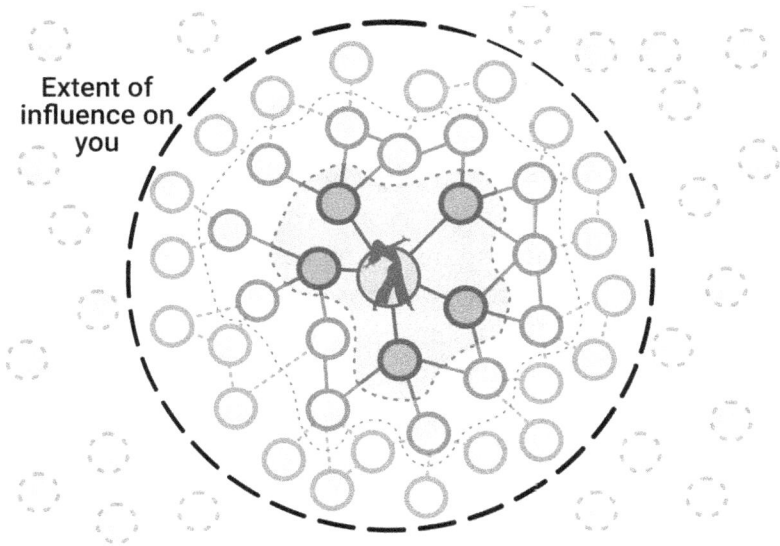

Extent of influence on you

Both deep and shallow networks are important. We can only maintain a relatively limited number of close relationships. We recognize the value of our closest connections with family, friends, and colleagues. And there is also great value in also being connected to a broader network of people. Breadth allows us to access a variety of information and hear about opportunities of different kinds. And being connected to different groups, even casually, can save us from getting caught in an echo chamber of people who look and think just like us.

From a career and business perspective, opportunities often come through people on the edge of our network. These people are likely to be connected to opportunities that we don't come across in our day-to-day interactions with those who we know well, who may share many of our own professional or business contacts.

Connecting with people who we don't know well is also beneficial for our wellbeing. Research by psychologist

Gillian Sandstrom showed that people report themselves as happier when they have casual interactions with other people throughout their day, for example through social activities or friendly conversations with staff in a coffee shop.[61] During the Covid-19 lockdown, many people struggled with the loss of these casual connections with other people. For me, reaching out to my network through Zoom meetings helped me to keep a sense of positivity and human connection. Proactively engaging with a network of other people is a valuable way to maintain a sense of purpose, connection, and support mental wellbeing.

An example is from The Royal Society for Arts Manufactures and Commerce (RSA). The RSA has a wide fellowship of members. Fellows share a common aim of helping to create a better future, through generating ideas and participating in practical initiatives with a social impact. The RSA supports a range of networks. During the Covid-19 lockdown in 2020, and beyond, their coaching network offered monthly meetings to anyone interested in coaching. The groups attracted people from all over the world, and I remember at one meeting having a beautiful heartfelt conversation with a coach from South Africa. A conversation that wouldn't have been possible without the facilitation of this group, and the wonders of Zoom.

Where can we find community?

Communities and networks are all around us once we start to look. Think about the networks and communities that you are part of, perhaps falling into some of the following categories.

Professional communities

Professionally, your network may start with the organization you work for, or your current clients if you're self-employed, as well as co-workers and clients from previous jobs. It may include people from professional networking clubs, membership bodies, or communities of practice. For example, I'm active in several communities and membership organizations for facilitators and coaches. These communities help members to connect with and learn from fellow professionals.

You may also be involved with organizations that bring people from different businesses or professions together to learn from and support each other in business development. Discovering the world of business networking was a game changer for me. Back in 2012 I attended my first networking meeting and realized that business networks can offer supportive, dynamic environments for connecting with others. They are popular among freelancers and sole traders as they help create a sense of community and reduce the isolation that can come with working alone. Some networking clubs are quite sales oriented, with an emphasis on referring business to each other. Others are more community focused; they may discourage overt selling in favour of relationship building, collaboration, and mutual support.

Glenda Shawley, MD of the Fabulous Networking community, has described her business as being like a flower garden. It's full of a variety of beautiful blooms, representing her members who are all different and unique. They want to grow personally and professionally. And as the gardener in this metaphor, Glenda provides a wide variety of different services that help to nurture and grow the flowers. She brings a caring vibe to her garden and loves seeing people flourish.

To make the most of your professional communities, it helps to be strategic in your approach. When working on my business plan for the year ahead, I think about which professional communities I want to be actively involved with. This tends to change over time as my business focus and professional interests evolve.

Local community initiatives

Many communities share a geographical link, such as people living in your village or street, or where people identify as being part of a group that share certain characteristics or perspectives.

Local community networks include your immediate neighbours, school communities, social clubs, and fundraising communities. In my town, for example, we have a hyper-local fundraising group that consists of local businesspeople, who organize events such as a biennial duck race and distribute the proceeds to local projects and individuals in need.

Many global or national organizations have local chapters, such as Rotary chapters across the world and Sierra Club chapters across the United States. Another example is Toastmasters International, a global not-for-profit educational organization that helps people develop public speaking and leadership skills through a worldwide network of clubs.[62]

Fellowship organizations such as Alcoholics Anonymous help people struggling with addictions to gain mutual support and mentoring from others in the same situation. Through an extensive network of groups, they draw on the power of peer support to help people make and sustain change. A high-profile advocate for these fellowships is comedian and activist Russell Brand, who has written about the 12-step recovery process in his book *Recovery*.[63]

Moving to Hampshire in 2008, I was heavily pregnant and without a local network of friends. The UK-based National Childbirth

Trust (NCT) offers classes to expectant parents. And as part of this, it actively encourages members of a class to stay in touch after their babies are born. It helps to establish a support and friendship network for people who really need it. I was grateful for this community at such a crucial time in my life, and for a while I also volunteered as a co-ordinator of an NCT group for new parents in my town.

Interest–based communities

Whatever your interest, there are likely to be communities built around it. Sporting or leisure activities, hobbies, politics, conservation, steam trains…

Social media offers a great starting point for finding communities, and once you start connecting with people who share your interests, you'll tap into recommendations and find many more. Since starting work on this book, I've become involved with three groups for writers. Each community offers something different, and together they've been sustaining and encouraging me throughout the process.

Another example is the TED Circles initiative, which ran formally from 2020 to 2022. The circles were volunteer-led groups, supported by resources from TED, which is a global non-profit organization devoted to spreading ideas, usually in the form of short, powerful talks.[64] Normally circles meet once a month, locally in person or via Zoom. Participants watch a TED talk together and use this as a starting point for a conversation. A simple format, but the richness of the talk can spark some inspiring and deep discussions. (TED Circles are now known as TED Members Group Discussions and are supported through the TED membership platform.[65])

Volunteering

Offering your time to help others in the community or to contribute to a cause is one of the best ways to connect with a purpose larger than yourself. Volunteering can offer a way to meet like-minded people and to live out your values. There is evidence that people who volunteer to help others are happier than those who don't,[66] and may even live longer.[67]

Practice: Mapping your network

Have you ever tried mapping your network? Grab a pen and paper and draw out those who you know. There may be a mix of individuals and groups within your map. Here are ideas for categories you might use:

- family, immediate and extended;
- friends, close friends, social circle, friendly acquaintances;
- social media friends;
- colleagues, working partners, and collaborators;
- former colleagues/collaborators;
- customers and clients – current and former;
- prospective customers;
- professional networking contacts;
- membership bodies and communities of professional practice;
- local community connections, e.g. via school, local businesses, voluntary work;
- communities of interest.

To enhance the visual impact of a network map, you could use proximity to show how deeply or superficially you know people. Or try a mind map, adapting the size of words or colours to show relative importance. Or use different sizes or placement of circles. What ways can you find to identify links and connections between different groups?

Mapping your network can be instructive. You may notice that you're connected to many people and organizations, in one way or another, but that most of these connections are quite superficial. In which case you might look for ways to deepen and develop some of these connections to build closer relationships.

Although there is value in having a wide network, you may find that your attention is being stretched too thinly. As a result, you might want to make a considered decision to let some of your connections go. For example, I'm a member of several professional membership organizations, and decided recently to leave one of them. I had been an active member earlier in my career, but this organization no longer felt as relevant to my work, and I decided that my level of commitment and involvement was not strong enough to be worth continuing.

Or you may feel that your network is too limited, and that you could do more to extend and broaden your involvement in networks and communities. Some thoughts on this are outlined below.

Seeking community

Getting involved with communities and networks can be enriching. Actively contributing to communities and networks can enhance your levels of happiness, health, and sense of purpose. And of course, the three-dimensional approach to seeking community is to start by connecting to yourself. Try asking yourself some simple questions.

What can you offer?

What can you bring to a network or community? Do you have relevant knowledge or skills? Can you offer support and encouragement?

What do you want?

And what would you like from the community? A community thrives through exchange and reciprocation. We have finite levels of time and energy to give, and community involvement should be a two-way process. For example, you may be giving time, but receiving a sense of satisfaction from living out your values in a positive way, to support others.

Where will you thrive?

In what environments or cultures do you thrive?

For example, I like participating in structured meetings where everyone has the chance to participate and no one is allowed to dominate. I'm happy to listen to someone talk non-stop in my professional coaching capacity, but within a network or social setting I don't want to attend an event dominated by a few voices (even my own!). When I'm facilitating, I aim to create the conditions for everyone to feel able to participate and share. And in turn, I appreciate being a participant in a meeting or event that's well facilitated by others. This is my perspective, and my preferences may not be yours. You may prefer a more informal atmosphere, for example, with minimal structure and more chatting and joking.

How do you feel?

A sign that you're involved with the right community or networking group for you is that you feel energized after getting together. If you find meetings draining or tiring, then reflect on the reasons why. Is it something about the group dynamic or culture that doesn't feel like a good fit for you? Or is it something that you are bringing to the experience, such as a negative expectation, that you could experiment with changing.

Summary: Crafting your network

- There is value in both deep connections and in a wider shallower network which can offer learning, opportunities, and a sense of community.
- A mapping exercise helps you to see where you already have strong connections, and in what parts of your professional or personal life you could extend or deepen your network.
- Community involvement has been shown to increase happiness, health, and a sense of purpose.
- Finding the right groups or communities is important, as different groups have different values, objectives, and dynamics. Ideally you will add value to the group, and in turn will be supported and energized.

Your perspective?

What communities and networks are you part of?

Are there people you would like to add to your network?

What professional membership organizations are most relevant to you at this stage in your career or business?

What groups or community initiatives could you get involved with?

There is a value in being part of a variety of networks, from professional membership organizations through to geographical and interest-based communities. Mapping your network and deciding where to focus your energies will help you to make the most of opportunities for connecting beyond your immediate circle. Weak ties may be particularly important when it comes to finding new career or business opportunities.

In the next chapter, we'll consider what to do if you can't find the right networks and communities to join, with ideas on starting your own initiatives.

Chapter 13

Crafting community Building valuable connections

Initiating community

It may be that you can't find local or professional communities or networking groups that feel like a good fit. If what you're looking for is not available, can you be part of starting something new? What could you do to reach out and set something in motion?

There are many ways to initiate community. It may be as simple as asking one or two people for a coffee, or offering to shop for a neighbour, as many people did during the Covid-19 lockdown period. Or it can be as substantial as setting up a new business or charitable organization to fill a perceived gap.

A useful question to start with is to decide whether you want to join forces with an existing initiative or organization, for example by starting up a local branch of a national group. Or whether you would prefer to start something completely new. This chapter includes some ideas for both joining and starting communities.

Partnering with an existing initiative

One way to start something in your community is to partner with an existing initiative that isn't currently represented in your area and instigate a new project or chapter. This could include volunteering through a charity or starting a new group within an established not-for-profit network. Or it might be linking with a commercial network, for example by buying a franchise. Going down this route will offer you structure and support to get something off the ground. Here are some ideas to get you thinking. Initiatives do tend to change over time, and these suggestions are correct at the time of writing.

The Eden Project's Big Lunch is a UK-wide initiative. To participate, you sign up as a volunteer. Then you receive guidance and promotional materials to help you host an annual outdoor lunch in June for people in your community: normally in the road where you live. The lunches are designed in the form of a bring-and-share street party. You may need to apply to close your road or find outdoor space in your street that's suitable for everybody. This can be a great way to get to know your neighbours and bring people together.

Lean In Circles are a global initiative set up by Sheryl Sandberg. Circles are led by volunteers who support women, and their allies, to come together to learn from each other, achieve goals, and be a positive force for change. Circles are free to attend, and can be held as in-person gatherings within a workplace setting, or in a community venue, or online. Lean In offers training, resources, and support for Circle Leaders.[68]

Another example of a volunteering-based initiative is run by the UK-based charity Action for Happiness, which offers opportunities for volunteers to run groups within community settings or online.[69] These groups help people reflect on how they can bring more happiness and resilience into their lives. You're bringing people together, but with resources and a support structure behind you, such as learning materials and help with promotion.

Business networking organizations are often looking for people to lead local groups. This may be on a voluntary basis, where you don't get paid, but you do get a higher profile within the group and potentially benefits such as complimentary membership. Or you may be looking at a franchise or licensing model where you purchase the right to run groups in a defined vicinity, and earn an income from your efforts.

Create your own network or community

If you can't find an existing initiative that appeals, maybe it's time to create your own. A starting point is to get imagining and thinking about what you might like to create, how you could achieve it, and whom you'd like to involve. The following questions may help.

What do you want to achieve?

It's difficult to bring an idea into reality without a clear sense of the purpose. Whether it's a walking club for local nature enthusiasts, a business club for mothers or a befriending service for older citizens, getting clarity on the purpose and benefits is an important first step. And so is building a picture of what you are aiming to achieve. To use the walking club as an example. How often will you walk? Where will you meet? Will the sessions be open to anyone, or would you like to offer sessions aimed at certain groups, for example carers or singles?

Is there a gap and a need?

Is there a need, desire, or appetite for a community initiative? Have you found a genuine gap that needs filling? You are likely to want to undertake some market research. A simple starting point could be a social media post or article to test the water and find out if there is any interest.

What strengths and skills do you bring?

What can you specifically bring to a community? This is about identifying your own skills and strengths. Are you a good organizer? Are you skilled at persuading people to join in and participate in activities? Are you able to facilitate engaging meetings? Being clear about your own strengths will help you decide where to focus your efforts, and to think about who else you could bring in at an early stage.

Who can help?

The next question is about whom you could collaborate with. There are plenty of examples of communities starting with an individual initiative, but it can also be very helpful to start with the support of another person or people. You can give each other moral support, share the workload, and bring complementary skills to a project.

Tips on starting a collaborative venture

If you're working collaboratively, ensure you have discussions early on about what you're trying to achieve and how it's going to work. Don't make assumptions; instead, make sure that you have talked the project through.

Capture agreements in writing. It doesn't necessarily need to be formal in tone, but even a few bullet points will be helpful in making sure you're on the same page and give you something to refer back to.

When collaborating on a project, don't only look at how well the venture is going, but also take time to review how you're working together. Allow any minor frustrations or potential areas of conflict to be aired as they arise; this heads off problems later on. Trust me on this!

Setting out expectations

In creating community, you may need to set some parameters and expectations about the way involvement will work. For example, are you looking for people to commit to regular attendance at meetings? Or are you happy for people to drop in? What is the level of confidentiality that you expect from members? Being clear about this will help people to know what is expected, so they can decide whether or not to get involved.

A healthy community is not rigid. Once people start to get involved, the community will change and shift. It will be dynamic; it will emerge and evolve as different people put in their ideas. So, think about the extent to which you want to set and maintain a framework for participation, versus the desire to not be too constricting. Finding a good balance between structure and openness will help enable a community or network to take off. If you try and exert too much control over it, then you may find people lose interest in staying involved, or the whole thing becomes quite cliquey and inward looking.

Even with a flexible approach, it's important to maintain some clear and values-based norms of behaviour, such as treating everybody with respect, regardless of their gender, ethnicity, or background. In the early days of developing a community, it's helpful to have open discussions about expectations and gather input. You can then capture these basic 'ground rules' in writing, and make sure founder members and new joiners have a copy. Review and revisit them from time to time to make sure the boundaries in place are working to foster and support a sense of community and connection.

Welcoming people in

How can you help people feel welcome and part of a community, network, or group, whilst at the same time holding some core values or ground rules? Being clear about the purpose and values of your group will tend to attract people for whom the group is a good fit. And it will help others to self-select themselves out.

The Fabulous Networking community is now run as a business, but it started life as a non-profit organization called Fabulous Women. Although a women-led network, men were always allowed to join. The ethos was inclusive. The community didn't seek to discriminate on gender, although the groups were built around what are sometimes considered feminine values such as sharing and collaboration. The current owner decided that the name wasn't welcoming enough to men, and the organization was rebranded whilst retaining its culture and values. The membership has since become much more gender balanced.

Size matters

Within any sort of community, as it grows, you're likely to see different levels of involvement, and different dynamics develop as numbers increase. I've found, in facilitating meetings, that above 12 people or so, the group will tend to dissipate into smaller groupings. You can use this to your advantage by deliberately setting up small group discussions within a larger meeting, mixing people around so they get to know a range of other people, rather than the same people clustering together all the time.

Anthropologist Robin Dunbar studied data from historic and current sources and found that there was a consistent pattern in how many people we can know in any meaningful sense.[70] The figure is around 150 people and is known as Dunbar's number. Of this, a much smaller number will form our circle of family relationships and our close friends. And beyond the 150, there is a wider circle of acquaintances, and a still wider network of people that we would recognize by sight. We may have hundreds of people that we know of through social media for example, but only on a very superficial level.

So, given that there is only a limited number of people we can truly connect with on a personal basis, it's important to be clear about which communities and connections are the most meaningful to us. We may wish to disengage from some communities and networks that no longer serve or inspire us, to allow time for us to connect with new ones.

Getting the word out

How will you let people know about your initiative? Finding ways to promote and advertise events or services is essential. The best place to start is with people you know who may be interested. But you'll also want to find ways to reach out beyond your existing friends and acquaintances.

Social media is an obvious route, and you may find the Nextdoor app is a good option for hyper-local events. Facebook local groups or interest groups can be helpful too. If there isn't an active relevant Facebook group, could you start one?

Meetup is also a good place to promote events that involve either face-to-face or online meetings. You pay a small amount to promote through Meetup but it has the benefit that people join this platform because they are specifically interested in making connections and finding events.

You could also approach other community organizations; local examples could be schools, Rotary Club, or similar, Chambers of Commerce, small business networks, parenting networks, etc. If you're offering something different to what's already in place, they might be happy to offer advice on what has worked for them or perhaps even promote your group to their members.

Also, you may consider placing an advertisement or writing an article in a relevant local or interest-based magazine. A good tip for advertising is to ensure that you have a place to capture people's interest so that you can approach them directly in the future. A good way to do this is via a webpage with an option to sign up for information and updates via email. Managing your email list via an opt-in mailing list provider will help you stay compliant with local data protection legislation.

A ripple...

If all this sounds like a lot of work, bear in mind that creating community doesn't mean you have to go to the lengths of setting up a group or an organization. You can make a difference by dropping a metaphorical pebble in the community pond and see how it ripples out. For example, you could offer to host a lunch for neighbours. Someone else might then be inspired to host an event another time. Setting something in motion is sometimes all that's needed for community to emerge.

And of course, there are myriad even smaller ways of building neighbourhood with your own community such as offering to feed a neighbour's pet when they are away. Even simple acts of support can increase a sense of community cohesion and ripple out. And to give you a work-related example, reaching out to one person to suggest a coffee or a Zoom conversation is a highly effective way to grow your professional network.

What if you start something and it doesn't really take off? This happens sometimes. Don't let that put you off trying again. It may be that the timing just isn't right or a different approach will bear fruit. And even if a community initiative is successful, it may draw to a natural close, as the dynamics of a group will shift and change over time. When a project is coming to a close, take time to celebrate the positive aspects and to acknowledge the ending.

Summary: Crafting community

- Joining or starting community initiatives can help fill gaps.
- Ways to initiate community include partnership with an established organization who can provide know-how and support. You can also explore whether there is an interest in something new using social media or simply reaching out to one person at a time.
- Getting clear about the purpose of your community or group will help you attract the right people.
- Make sure you allow plenty of time for publicity to get the word out.
- Celebrate success and acknowledge endings when they come.

Your perspective?

Is there something missing in your local, professional, or interest-based community?

If you would like to start an initiative, with whom could you collaborate?

What might be the purpose of your initiative: what would you like to achieve and who could benefit from being involved?

How could you expand your professional or social community, one person at a time?

In this chapter we've looked at ways to craft community. A starting point is to clarify your purpose and what you'd like to achieve. There are many ways to turn ideas into action, which may include joining or starting an initiative to bring people together. Or you may focus on taking small steps to build your individual connections with people in your community.

In the next chapter we take an expanded view and think about the experience of interconnection, and how we can develop our own sense of being more connected to the wider whole, of which we are an integral part.

Chapter 14

Beyond the self
The art and practice of
interconnection

An experience of interconnection

Thirty of us gather on the smooth wooden floor of a Latin dance club in Southampton. But we're not dancing Latin grooves today. Instead, we are gathered to move together to music, chosen to take us on a dance journey. We are invited to tune in to our bodies; to connect with the movements in our hands and wrists, shoulders, head, torso, hips, knees, feet... We connect into our bodies and follow our own movements. There are no steps to learn, there's nothing we can get wrong; we are invited to tune in to how we want to move, to move in a way that feels good and respects our own physical potential and limitations.

As the class progresses, we may connect with another person and move together. Not in a formal partner dance; instead, we're allowing another person to witness our dance as we witness theirs. We allow ourselves to be inspired by another's dance. Maybe we are struck by something the other person is doing: a specific move or a quality that they bring to their movement. We allow them to influence our own dance, whilst still maintaining awareness of our self, of our own movement, of our own body, only moving what is comfortable for us to move. And we connect with different individuals, all dancing and moving in their own way, their unique responses to a shared rhythm.

At times we may extend our awareness to the whole room. We look out and see 30 dancing bodies. Human beings just like us. And as we all dance and move, we give each other implicit permission to dance and move in our own way. Some people dance more slowly, gently, maybe even seated. Others move to the centre of the room and gyrate more energetically. All moving within the constraints of our own bodies but forming part of a group experience.

The dance of life

This experience of dancing freely has been one of the most transformative experiences in my life. I started my conscious dance journey through the work of Gabrielle Roth,[71] and more recently I've discovered other free movement approaches, including Nia FreeDance,[72] Movement Medicine,[73] and Biodanza.[74]

All these experiences give me a sense of being truly alive. They facilitate a felt sensation of being deeply connected with myself, of being aware of others, and of feeling in community with other people. There have even been moments where I seem to sense the whole pulsating shifting dance of life, catch a glimpse of transcendence and feel part of the whole interconnected matrix of life.

It's not to say dancing always feels like this. Sometimes it feels more effortful or there's a sense of not being fully tuned in to the group experience. But I've found that if I just keep going and keep moving through the sense of stuckness, it will change into something else. Like any kind of practice, if it's worthwhile and you keep doing it, it will bring its rewards.

Paths to interconnection

Dance may not be the path for you, and my invitation is to reflect on what gives you or might give you a sense of connecting beyond.

Some people describe a similar sense of connection and expansion through singing in a choir or playing in a band or orchestra. Not necessarily professionally; it's more about gathering with others to sing or play as a group. Listening, expressing, and together creating something that is more than the individual voices or instruments.

The use of movement and voice to create a sense of connection and expanded awareness is sometimes used by motivational speakers. Members of the audience may be encouraged to move or dance or sing, and this helps create an experience for many of an altered or expanded awareness, and the potential for letting go of some of your everyday concerns.

For some people, this kind of togetherness is of course found within a religious context. Gathering and singing in a religious setting can offer this sense of making sound with other people, in a joint recognition of the transcendent, experienced through a communal belief in the deity being worshipped.

And perhaps the most widely appreciated and powerful way that humans connect beyond the self is through spending time in nature. The cycles of nature, the process of birth and decay, the ever-changing interplay of elements, all give us a sense of being part of something. There is a Japanese term *shinrin-yoku*, which means 'bathing in the forest atmosphere', and research evidence demonstrates tangible health benefits of spending time in nature and around trees. Forest bathing expert Dr Qing Li recommends taking two hours in nature, unplugged, and using all your senses to take in the sounds, smells, and images around you. Touch plants, trees, and the earth, drink in and taste the freshness of the air.[75]

Another proven way to feel more connected is to volunteer, to give your time to help others. Volunteering can increase happiness and a sense of purpose. It can range from offering informal support for a neighbour through to a regular commitment to give time to an organization. It can mean sharing specialist skills or just pitching in to help out for an event.

Feeling a strong sense of interconnection is often a temporary experience, as a shift in our neurochemistry gives us a different perspective on the world. But if you do these kinds of practices regularly, it can build up your sense of expanded awareness that we're all part of a bigger whole, and allow that to permeate into your everyday life.

The illusion of individuality

In the west, our cultural history has prompted a way of seeing ourselves as individuals. And yes, of course, on one level we are a separate organism. Most of us, unless we are suffering from some forms of mental illness, notably dementia, have a sense of selfhood that persists from childhood through to old age. This is important to our sense of who we are, our fundamental connection with ourselves. Some powerful psychological approaches such as psychosynthesis, developed by Roberto Assagioli,[76] emphasize the importance of accepting and integrating different aspects of ourselves, thus maintaining a coherent sense of self whilst not over-identifying with any one aspect of our personality.

But you don't need to think about it for long to realize that our individuality is also to some extent an illusion. The physical components of our bodies change from minute to minute as we breathe in and out. Our bodies and brains do not contain any of the atoms that they did ten years ago. Our memories are patterns that give us a sense of connection with our past selves, but that self is gone, and the atoms that used to be in us are now elsewhere: in another person, in a plant, in an animal…

We are not separate from the natural world; we are part of it. Our cultural tendency to view the world as under our control has given us benefits in terms of comfort and convenience, through the practical applications of science and technology. It has also extracted a steep price as millions suffer from the effects of pollution, forest fires rage, and coral reefs die. Unless we learn to respect nature and recognize that we are part of nature, we are unlikely to thrive or maybe even survive. For most people, what really matters are connection and relationships, and any meaningful future needs to put these front and centre. We are connected to all life and what we do matters as our impact ripples out.

Scientifically and ecologically, life is process.[77] The world is a constantly shifting matrix of interconnection and as human beings we are interconnected too. As psychologist Carl Rogers identified, we are persons in the process of becoming; we are never done.[78] Modern neuroscience explains how when we remember, we reconstruct our memories each time. Our memories aren't stored in our brains as rice in a jar; we literally re-member, which means: put parts together again. We may even use different neuropathways each time we reconstruct a memory,[79] so it's no wonder our memories shift and change too. The criminal justice system knows this unreliability of memory only too well, as they interview witnesses to an event and try to build a picture from different accounts. And this ability to change memories can be used in a positive way, as we can review events from the past that may be painful and look at them with a different, maybe kinder, perspective.

What matters to most people at the end of their lives is their relationships, and the extent to which they were able to be themselves. In learning more about ourselves, we can realize our own unique individuality, and at the same time recognize our common humanity and our connection to all life.

We are pattern-making animals, who need to make meaning from events in our lives and to find life meaning-full. Sometimes it's about finding meaning in our place in the society or community or family in which we find ourselves. It's in the roles we play in relation to others.

Sometimes it's the meaning we construct through making sense of our journey through life. The story of how we arrived at where we are now. And the story projected into the future of where we'll end up.

There's also potentially meaning to be found in the sense of the vastness of the universe in which we find ourselves. Who hasn't at some point looked up at a clear night sky and felt a sense of awe? We can witness the vastness without necessarily needing to have a particular role other than that of witness. We can expand our perspective to encompass a world in which we are part of the kaleidoscope of shifting changing patterns. We can be both the witness and the witnessed. We can see ourselves as part of the much greater story in which what came before and what comes after is within us for a short while until the great dance of life moves on again.

I believe we all need to find a philosophy of life that gives us a sense of meaning or purpose. For some, this may be the belief, rituals, and community found within a formal religion. For others, it may be a meaning that we have had to weave for ourselves. My personal sense of meaning incorporates everything I've learnt to date about subjects including dance, psychology, philosophy, mindfulness, neuroscience, leadership, and metaphor. It needs to somehow synthesize the specific and eclectic mix of knowledge, experience, and understanding that is the sum total of my 50-plus years of living and learning. And I want to be open to continually changing and updating my understanding of the world as I learn and experience more.

What's true for me at the point of writing this cannot possibly be exactly what is true for you. And it won't be what's still true for me if I pick up this book again in ten years' time. My hope is that this writing has given you some ideas, inspiration, practices or provocations that will help you in your own journey of making meaning and connection with yourself and others.

Practices: Interconnecting

Everyday interconnection

Take time during your day-to-day activities to pause and reflect on the multiple levels of interconnection that support you. Every time you go to the supermarket, you are interacting with a whole supply chain of people, and beyond that there may be the animals or plants that contributed to even one everyday product. When you go online, the interconnections include those who devised and developed the internet, the devices and electricity that make access possible, and those who produced the informative, commercial, or social sites that you visit.

Do more of what works

Think about what makes your life experience feel expanded, interconnected, and meaningful for you. And do more of it!

Try something new

I've shared a few of my personal favourite transformational practices throughout this book, and in the accompanying *Connection Craft Kit* (details on page 212).

Summary: Crafting interconnection

- We are all interconnected: with other people, with the non-human living world, and with the elements that make up the building blocks of our physical reality.
- Feeling connected beyond the self can offer a sense of meaning and purpose.
- There are different paths to experiencing a sense of connecting beyond the self, and an art to finding an approach that allows you to experience this interconnection.

Your perspective?

What helps you feel connected to the wider whole?

What makes life feel meaningful for you?

In this chapter you've considered the wider context in which you live your life, and how appreciation of myriad interconnections can contribute to a sense of meaning.

We'll return to the *Connecting in 3D* model in the next chapter to consider how the three levels connect and weave together as we craft connection in our personal and professional lives.

Chapter 15

Conclusion
Connecting in 3D,
PARED down

Connecting in 3D is a holistic, layered approach to connection and communication.

It starts with an appreciation of your own being. It involves an awareness of your inner sensations and the ability to take different perspectives. This includes being able to orient yourself in time, to see your story from fresh vantage points, and to take an observer view of your own thought processes. It asks you to integrate the wisdom and messages from your body with your logical thinking mind, and to identify your values and integrate them into the way you make decisions and live your life.

The second dimension is about connecting with others, whilst retaining a sense of connection with self. It involves participating in a dialogue, with an equal respect for yourself and others. It requires an understanding of your own reactions to other people's words and behaviours. And at the heart of real connection is a willingness, intention, and ability to listen deeply to another person, to what they say and what is left unsaid, with sensitivity to their words, voice, and body language, and to respond accordingly.

The third layer takes into account the wider tapestry of life, of which we are each a part. We all stand at the centre of our own circle. And yet we are linked to other people and to the ecology of the planet itself. Communities and networks emerge from the dynamic interactions of people, philosophies, beliefs, dialogue, and actions. We are not static, unchanging beings, but are always in the process of becoming. Gaining a sense of our place in the tapestry of life can provide a sense of meaning, which will be entirely individual, yet recognizes that, on some level, we are all connected.

Weaving through these three dimensions, we are always connecting in different ways. Sometimes we're inner-focused, sometimes our attention is on listening to another, and sometimes we're open to the wider connectivity of which we are a part. If we allow them, these three levels can support each other to give us a richer experience of life, and allow us to touch the lives of others more deeply.

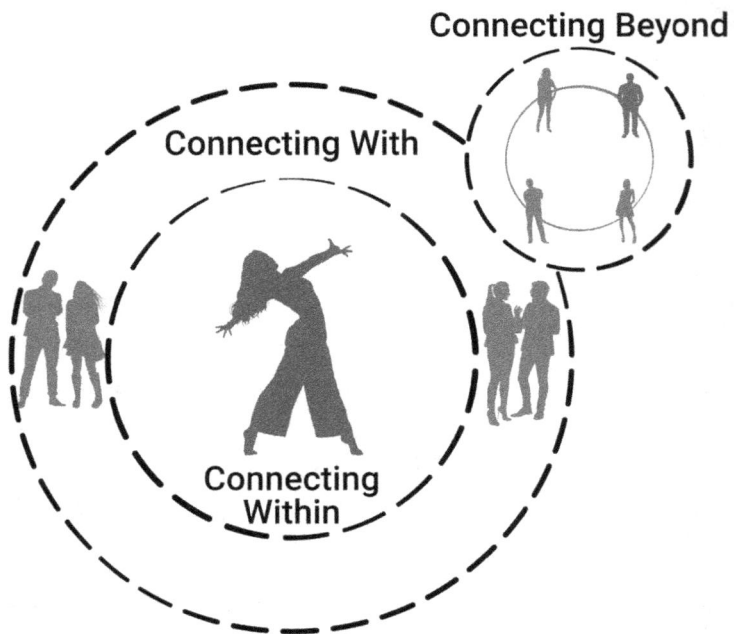

Connecting Beyond

Connecting With

Connecting Within

As our journey through *Connecting in 3D* draws to a close, I would like to offer you a PARED-down summary of key ideas in this book. PARED stands for: Presence, Awareness, Respect, Exchange, Dynamic.

Presence

This is the skill of bringing your attention back to the present moment to recognize where you are in time and space. It's the ability to be aware of yourself, whilst staying in connection with another person. You can develop your ability to return to the present through practices such as mindfulness. And one of the quickest ways for most people to reset is through connecting with an immediate physical sensation such as the feeling of your feet on the floor or the temperature of the skin on your hands.

Acceptance

Becoming increasingly accepting of your own thoughts and feelings helps you to acknowledge uncomfortable emotions without being overwhelmed by them. And an openness to accepting that others have different viewpoints, based on their own individual histories, physiology, and stories, makes it easier to listen without judgement.

Respect

Respecting yourself and others provides a foundation for authentic connection. Respecting yourself means acknowledging that you have as much right to be heard as anyone else. And respect for others is about seeing the other person as equal to you, as a human being. You may agree or disagree with someone's views, whilst respecting them as a person and recognizing that conflict doesn't need to affect your ability to empathize with others, as you try to understand why they think and feel as they do.

Exchange

Exchange is part of the reciprocal nature of a conversation, as we both listen and speak. A worthwhile conversation between two or more people results in a shared meaning emerging through the exchange. We empathize with others, and add our own thoughts and ideas to build on or challenge what has gone before. And connection facilitates healthy exchange, such as exchanging feedback, exchanging time, exchanging attention or exchanging knowledge.

Dynamic

Nothing is static. When we connect in with ourselves, we recognize that our thoughts and feelings change, we can grow in self-awareness, and we have the capacity to learn and develop throughout our lives. When we connect with others, we create a dynamic system; as we listen to understand, our own thinking is stimulated, and new insights, distinctions, perspectives, or meaning can emerge directly from the interactions. A conversation can start a movement which can change the world.

The power of connection

In a world where we have never had so much access to other people, through the power of the internet and social media, it can sometimes feel that we are becoming more atomized. We may find ourselves sitting alone, consuming content online. Or we may put our own ideas on the internet, not knowing who will see them, perhaps with the hope of receiving likes or shares. This might give us a fleeting sense of being acknowledged by others, but for most of us, this isn't the kind of deep connection that nourishes our lives.

In this book I've tried to share a model of connection that starts within and reaches out, that feels deeper and more authentic. As a child I often felt like an outsider, moving from school to school, never feeling fully part of a community. And the practices shared in this book are ones that have helped me build a sense of deep connection and sense of joy that has become a natural state of being. I am happy in my own company and enjoy the company of other people, bringing a sense of interest and curiosity to conversations. And when I'm experiencing a bad day, I know to draw on some of the practices in this book to shift my emotions and get back into a state of appreciation for being part of something bigger than myself. This, in turn, brings a more positive energy to the way I'm able to interact with others.

Ultimately, feeling connected is an inside job. You can feel a sense of connection when you're alone, just as you can feel disconnected within a crowd. Exploring what helps you feel connected within is the starting point for deeper, more authentic relationships, and can help you bring more meaning and purpose to all aspects of your life.

Connection Craft Kit – my gift to you

I've put together a complimentary Connection Craft Kit for you, to support you in integrating the ideas in this book. Your craft kit includes:

- Companion workbooks, with key ideas and reflective questions
- Supplementary audio, video, and downloadable PDF resources
- Felicity's Little Black Book of Transformational Practices

Please visit https://felicitydwyer.com/craft-kit

Connecting with you

As this chapter closes, please do stay connected if you'd like to. You can find me at www.felicitydwyer.com. And in the spirit of dialogue, I'd love to hear your thoughts and reflections on the ideas raised in this book. You can contact me via my website, find me on LinkedIn, or comment on my blog.

With respect and appreciation,

Felicity

Selected bibliography

Booker, C. (2004). *The Seven Basic Plots: Why We Tell Stories*, Continuum.

Boyd, J. and Zimbardo, P. (2010). *The Time Paradox: Using the New Psychology of Time to Your Advantage*, Rider.

Christakis, N. A. and Fowler, J. H. (2009). *Connected: The Amazing Power of Social Networks and How They Shape Our Lives*, Little, Brown.

Darling-Khan, S. and Darling-Khan, Y. (2009). *Movement Medicine: How to Awaken, Dance and Live Your Dreams*, Hay House.

Dass, R. (1971, 1978). *Be Here Now, Remember*, Hanuman Foundation.

Feldman Barrett, L. (2020). *Seven and a Half Lessons about the Brain*, Picador.

Ferrucci, P. (2000). *What We May Be: The Vision and Techniques of Psychosynthesis*, Tarcher/Putnam.

Fox Cabane, O. (2012). *The Charisma Myth*, Portfolio/Penguin.

Gladwell, M. (2006). *Blink: The Power of Thinking Without Thinking*, Penguin.

Goleman, D., Boyatzis, R., and McKee, A. (2002). *The New Leaders: Transforming the Art of Leadership into the Science of Results*, Little, Brown.

Harari, Y. H. (2011, 2014). *Sapiens: A Brief History of Humankind*, Vintage.

Harari, Y. H. (2018). *21 Lessons for the 21st Century*, Vintage.

Harris, R. (2011, 2019). *The Confidence Gap: From Fear to Freedom*, Robinson.

Harris, R. (2022). *The Happiness Trap: Stop Struggling, Start Living*, 2nd ed., Robinson.

Klein, G. (2004). *The Power of Intuition: How to Use Your Gut Feelings to Make Better Decisions at Work*, Random House.

Kline, N. (1999). *Time to Think: Listening to Ignite the Human Mind*, Cassell.

Kline, N. (2020). *The Promise That Changes Everything: I Won't Interrupt You*, Penguin.

Lakoff, G. and Johnson, M. (2003). *Metaphors We Live By*, University of Chicago Press.

Lawley, J. D. and Tomkins, P. L. (2002). *Metaphors in Mind: Transformation Through Symbolic Modelling*, Developing Company Press.

Lovatt, P. (2018). *Dance Psychology*, Fine Printing.

Oliver, J., Hill, J., and Morris, E. (2015). *ACTivate Your Life: Using Acceptance and Mindfulness to Build a Life That Is Rich, Fulfilling and Fun*, Robinson.

Oliver, T. (2020). *The Self Delusion: The Surprising Science of Our Connection to Each Other and the Natural World*, Weidenfeld & Nicolson.

Parker, P. (2018). *The Art of Gathering: How We Meet and Why It Matters*, Penguin.

Rodenburg, P. (1992, 2005). *The Right to Speak: Working with the Voice*, Methuen.

Rogers, C. R. (1961). *On Becoming a Person: A Therapist's View of Psychotherapy*, Robinson.

Rogers, C. R. (1980). *A Way of Being*, Houghton Mifflin.

Rosas, D. and Rosas, C. (2004). *The Nia Technique: The High-Powered Energising Workout That Gives You a New Body and a New Life*, Harmony.

Roth, G. (2003). *Maps to Ecstasy: The Healing Power of Movement,* 2nd ed., New World Library.

Schein, E. H. (2016). *Organizational Culture and Leadership*, 5th ed., Wiley.

Soosalu, G. and Oka, M. (2012). *mBraining: Using Your Multiple Brains to Do Cool Stuff*, mBIT International.

Sullivan, W. and Rees, J. (2008). *Clean Language Revealing Metaphors and Opening Minds,* Crown House.

Syed, M. (2019). *Rebel Ideas: The Power of Diverse Thinking*, John Murray.

Way, M. (2013). *Clean Approaches for Coaching: How to Create the Conditions for Change Using Clean Language and Symbolic Modelling*, Clean Publishing.

Acknowledgements

Firstly, thank you to Sophia, my beautiful daughter. You are my greatest teacher, and you show me everything I have yet to learn about crafting connection. I love you.

And my wholehearted appreciation goes to all who have helped me in my book-writing journey. This endeavour has taught me that writing a book is a collaborative process. I've found a wellspring of support and encouragement from friends and colleagues, and have made wonderful new connections along the way. I've greatly valued your feedback, encouragement, challenges, and suggestions.

Thank you to the amazing Alison Jones at Practical Inspiration who has supported and guided me at every stage of this journey, and to all the team who have been so helpful with editing and design, including Lizzie Evans and her team at Newgen, development editors Kate Llewellyn and Géraldine Collard for their insightful suggestions, Katie Finnegan for copy-editing the final draft, and Judith Wise for her help with publicity and promotion.

Thank you to all the members of the Fabulous Networking Book Challenge group, and those who attend Alison's Extraordinary Business Book Club Campfire sessions, for the encouragement and learning along the way. A special shout-out to Glenda Shawley, who does so much to support her Fabulous Networking community and has been a cheerleader throughout the whole process. And a particular thank you to those who gave me feedback on early drafts and helped me feel both that the book was worth writing, and how it could be improved. Thank you to Angela Marshall, Liz Gresson, Nick Keith, and

Glenda Shawley. And another special mention for Nick Keith – it was after a talk that you gave on writing at Fabulous Networking Eastleigh that I came up with the initial idea for this book. Thanks also to Lucy Boyland and Marian Way who gave me helpful pointers for Chapters 4 and 8, respectively. I've taken on board much of the constructive feedback that I was given from you all, and of course any errors or omissions are entirely down to me!

I'm deeply thankful to all of you who were kind enough to read the final draft of this book and write an endorsement, published at the front of the book; I appreciate your kind words and willingness to support this endeavour. Thank you to Angela, Sarah, Glenda, Nick, Graham, Jess, Liz, Krista, and Jeremy.

Many wise teachers have helped me learn and develop the ideas that have gone into this book. There's no way that I can acknowledge you all, but here I would like to say thank you to Marian Way at Clean Learning for opening my mind to the power of Clean Language and helping me gain my Clean Facilitator certification, Elisa Risquez and Dorit Noble for introducing me to the body of work that is Nia, Nicola Humber for her illuminating Unbound Writing approach, Maggie Piazza for believing in me and my potential, Jacqui McGinn for being a constant inspiration, and Shirley Wardell, my teacher and supervisor on the Time to Think Facilitator accreditation. And to all the wonderful dance and movement teachers that I've learnt from over the years, including Sue Rickards, Malcolm Stern, Gay Murphy, Ruth Hirst, Ajay Rajani, Georgina Watts, Ya'Acov and Susannah Darling-Khan, amongst many others.

I've been fortunate to experience insightful coaching and thinking time over the past year with some extraordinarily skilled people, including Laura Murphy, Mindy Gibbins-Klein, Jess Annison, Kate Hardy, and Alison Jones, all of whom helped me think through ideas and identify practical actions towards realisation of this book.

And last, but emphatically not least, my heartfelt thanks to Mike Clayton for your illustrations, and for your honest and incredibly helpful feedback on this writing journey. You are a powerhouse, and I am forever learning from you.

About the author

Felicity Dwyer is a facilitator, trainer, coach, and speaker. She helps individuals and teams to connect and communicate, so that people feel heard and understood. Her style is warm, engaging, and inclusive. Felicity's clients include national and local charities, public sector organizations, and small businesses.

With over 20 years' experience in facilitating personal and professional development for individuals and groups, she also has expertise in coaching people through professional transitions. Felicity is an experienced trainer and assessor for both CMI and ILM leadership and management qualifications and delivers workshops on communication skills topics such as assertiveness, presentation skills, handling difficult conversations, and managing change. As a speaker, she has presented at conferences and seminars across the UK.

She is a certified Clean Language Facilitator, Time to Think Facilitator and Nia White Belt, and holds qualifications and certifications in coaching skills, training practice, person-centred counselling, management and leadership, and the neuroscience of change.

Felicity's lifelong commitment to personal development and learning has encompassed many transformative practices, including conscious dance, psychosynthesis, and symbolic modelling. The practices that she uses in her personal life and shares through her workshops and coaching are evidence based, creative, and effective, and she teaches them in a practical and accessible way.

You can learn about ways to work with Felicity on her website: www.felicitydwyer.com

Endnotes

[1] Fox Cabane, O. (2012). *The Charisma Myth*, Portfolio/Penguin.

[2] Boyd, J. and Zimbardo, P. (2010). *The Time Paradox: Using the New Psychology of Time to Your Advantage*, Rider.

[3] Blake, W., stanzas from 'Auguries of Innocence' (published 1863), cited in *Poets of the English Language* (1950), Viking. Available from www.poetryfoundation.org/poems/43650/auguries-of-innocence [accessed 12 May 2022].

[4] Mindful Communications, 'What is mindfulness?' Available from www.mindful.org/what-is-mindfulness/ [accessed 12 May 2022].

[5] American Psychological Association, 'What are the benefits of mindfulness'. Available from www.apa.org/monitor/2012/07-08/ce-corner [accessed 12 May 2022].

[6] Zuckerman, A. (2020). '46 meditation statistics: 2020/2021 benefits, market value & trends'. *CompareCamp*, 22 May 2020. Available from https://comparecamp.com/meditation-statistics/ [accessed 12 May 2022].

[7] David Treleaven, PhD, is a leading trainer for trauma-sensitive mindfulness practitioners: https://davidtreleaven.com

[8] I first learnt this technique from Russ Harris on his ACT for Beginners programme.

[9] Dass, R. (1971, 1978). *Be Here Now, Remember*, Hanuman Foundation.

[10] Herculano-Houzel, S. (2012). 'The remarkable, yet not extraordinary human brain as a scaled-up primate brain and its associated cost'. *PNAS*. Available from www.pnas.org/content/109/Supplement_1/10661 [accessed 12 May 2022].

[11] Underwood, E. (2018). 'Your gut is directly connected to your brain, by a newly discovered neuron circuit'. *Science*, 20 September 2018. Available from www.science.org/content/article/your-gut-directly-connected-your-brain-newly-discovered-neuron-circuit [accessed 12 May 2022].

[12] Alshami, A. M. (2019). 'Pain: Is it all in the brain or the heart?' *Current Pain and Headache Reports*, 23(12), 88. https://doi.org/10.1007/s11916-019-0827-4

[13] Soosalu, G., Henwood, S., and Deo, A. (2019). 'Head, heart, and gut in decision making: Development of a multiple brain preference questionnaire'. *SAGE Open*, 9(1). https://doi.org/10.1177%2F2158244019837439

[14] 'The 90 second life cycle of an emotion'. Available from www.youtube.com/watch?v=vxARXvljKBA [accessed 12 May 2022].

[15] Klein, G. (2003). *The Power of Intuition*, Random House.

[16] I am grateful to coach and author Jeremy Glyn for introducing me to this technique. It comes from the field of applied kinesiology, originated by Dr. George Goodheart, Jr.

[17] HeartMath Institute: www.heartmath.org

[18] Oppezzo, M. and Schwartz, D. L. (2014). 'Give your ideas some legs: The positive effect of walking on creative thinking'. *Journal of Experimental Psychology: Learning, Memory, and Cognition*, 40(4), 1142–1152. Available from www.apa.org/pubs/journals/releases/xlm-a0036577.pdf [accessed 12 May 2022].

[19] Campion and Levita (2014), cited in Lovatt, P. (2018) *Dance Psychology*, Fine Printing.

[20] Lovatt, P. (2018). *Dance Psychology*, Fine Printing.

[21] Steiner, S. (2012). 'Top five regrets of the dying'. *The Guardian*, 1 February 2012. Available from www.theguardian.com/

lifeandstyle/2012/feb/01/top-five-regrets-of-the-dying [accessed 12 May 2022].

22 Schein, E. H. (2016). *Organizational Culture and Leadership*, 5th ed., Wiley.

23 Goleman, D., Boyatzis, R. E., and McKee, A. (2001). 'Primal leadership: The hidden driver of great performance'. *Harvard Business Review*, December 2001. Available from https://hbr.org/2001/12/primal-leadership-the-hidden-driver-of-great-performance [accessed 12 May 2022].

24 I came across the concept of defusion in studying ACT – Acceptance and Commitment Therapy. ACT is an evidence-based cognitive approach to living a psychologically healthy and meaningful life. ACT includes ideas about defusing from uncomfortable thoughts and feelings as one of the six components of psychological flexibility. Other principles from ACT include acceptance and values-guided action.

25 Mind (2019). 'Dissociation and dissociative disorders'. Available from www.mind.org.uk/information-support/types-of-mental-health-problems/dissociation-and-dissociative-disorders/about-dissociation/ [accessed 12 May 2022].

26 Jung, C. G. (1933). *Modern Man in Search of a Soul*, Kegan Paul, Trench, Trüber & Co., pp. 234–235.

27 Feldman Barrett, L. (2021). 'Variation is the stuff of life. So why can it make us uncomfortable?' Available from www.theguardian.com/commentisfree/2021/mar/04/variation-uncomfortable-embracing-difference-success-species [accessed 9 August 2021].

28 Lakoff, G. and Johnson, M. (2003). *Metaphors We Live By*, University of Chicago Press.

29 Symbolic modelling is a process developed by James Lawley and Penny Tomkins, drawing on the work of therapist David Grove.

The method is used in therapy and coaching to draw in conscious awareness of the metaphors that influence people's experience of the world. See https://cleanlanguage.co.uk for a wealth of information on this subject.

[30] I trained as a Clean Facilitator with Marian Way at Clean Learning. The Clean Learning website includes a list of qualified facilitators: https://cleanlearning.co.uk/about/facilitators

[31] From Steve Jobs' Commencement address, Stanford University, 12 June 2005. Stanford News (2005), "'You've got to find what you love,' Job says'. Available from https://news.stanford.edu/2005/06/14/jobs-061505/ [accessed 12 May 2022].

[32] Kline, N. (1999). *Time to Think: Listening to Ignite the Human Mind*, Cassell.

[33] Fox, K. (2005). *Watching the English: The Hidden Rules of English Behaviour*, Hodder & Stoughton.

[34] Kline, N. (2012). *Time to Think Facilitator's Manual*. Also see Time to Think (2020). 'The ten components'. Available from www.timetothink.com/thinking-environment/the-ten-components/ [accessed 12 May 2022].

[35] Rogers, C. R. (1961). *On Becoming a Person: A Therapist's View of Psychotherapy*, Robinson.

[36] Rogers, C. R. (1980). *A Way of Being*, Houghton Mifflin, p. 143.

[37] Cambridge Dictionary (2022). Definition of 'assertive'. Available from https://dictionary.cambridge.org/dictionary/english/assertive [accessed 12 May 2022].

[38] Quote Investigator (2012). 'No one can make you feel inferior without your consent'. Available from https://quoteinvestigator.com/2012/04/30/no-one-inferior/ [accessed 12 May 2022].

[39] The *5 Whys* technique was originally developed by Sakichi Toyoda: https://en.wikipedia.org/wiki/Five_whys [accessed 11 August 2021].

[40] Forleo, M. (2019). *Everything is Figureoutable*, Penguin.

[41] Grove, D. J. and Panzer, B. I. (1991). *Resolving Traumatic Memories: Metaphors and Symbols in Psychotherapy*, Irvington Publishers Inc.

[42] Lawley, J. D. and Tomkins, P. L. (2002). *Metaphors in Mind: Transformation Through Symbolic Modelling*, Developing Company Press.

[43] Booker, C. (2004). *The Seven Basic Plots: Why We Tell Stories*, Continuum.

[44] I first came across this two-phase approach in a storytelling workshop at the Larmer Tree Festival.

[45] TED talks. Available from www.ted.com/talks [accessed 12 May 2022].

[46] Miller, D. (2017). *Building a StoryBrand: Clarify Your Message So Customers Will Listen*, Thomas Nelson.

[47] Hickel, J. (2020). *Less is More: How Degrowth Will Save the World*, Heinemann, pp. 68–69.

[48] Data Science at Home (2019). 'The dark side of AI: Social media and the optimization of addiction'. Podcast episode, 3 December 2019. Available from https://datascienceathome.com/the-dark-side-of-ai-social-media-and-the-optimization-of-addiction/ [accessed 12 May 2022].

[49] Hartman, J. (2020). 'Whose metaphor? Autism Spectrum Disorder and metaphorization'. *MetNet Scandinavia*, 7 May 2020. Available from www.metnetscandinavia.com/post/whose-metaphor-autism-spectrum-disorder-and-metaphorization [accessed 12 May 2022].

[50] Goodreads. 'Jean-Luc Godard: "Sometimes reality is too complex. Stories give it form"'. Available from www.goodreads.com/quotes/514541-sometime-reality-is-too-complex-stories-give-it-form [accessed 12 May 2022].

[51] British Library. 'Albert Mehrabian'. Available from www.bl.uk/people/albert-mehrabian [accessed 12 May 2022].

[52] Paul Ekman Group (2022). 'Micro expressions'. Available from www.paulekman.com/resources/micro-expressions/ [accessed 12 May 2022].

[53] Wikipedia (2022). 'Microexpression'. Available from https://en.wikipedia.org/wiki/Microexpression [accessed 12 May 2022].

[54] Rodenburg, P. (1992, 2005). *The Right to Speak: Working with the Voice*, Methuen.

[55] Collins Dictionary (2022). Definition of 'feedback'. Available from www.collinsdictionary.com/dictionary/english/feedback [accessed 12 May 2022].

[56] Luft, J. and Ingham, H. (1955). 'The Johari window: A graphic model of interpersonal awareness'. *Proceedings of the Western Training Laboratory in Group Development*, University of California.

[57] Bolton, G. (2010). *Reflective Practice: Writing and Professional Development*, 3rd ed., Sage.

[58] Definition of 'network'. Available from www.merriam-webster.com/dictionary/network [accessed 12 May 2022].

[59] Granovetter, M. S. (1973). 'The strength of weak ties'. *American Journal of Sociology*, 78(6), 1360–1380. Available from https://snap.stanford.edu/class/cs224w-readings/granovetter73weakties.pdf [accessed 12 May 2022].

[60] Christakis, N. A. and Fowler, J. H. (2009). *Connected: The Amazing Power of Social Networks and How They Shape Our Lives,* Little, Brown, pp. 50–51.

[61] Department of Psychology, University of Cambridge (2014). 'Talking to strangers might make you happier: Dr Gillian Sandstrom's research covered in New York Times'. Available from www.psychol. cam.ac.uk/news/gillian-sandstrom [accessed 12 May 2022].

[62] Toastmasters (2022). 'All about Toastmasters'. Available from www. toastmasters.org/about/all-about-toastmasters [accessed 9 August 2021].

[63] Brand, R. (2018). *Recovery: Freedom from Our Addictions*, Bluebird.

[64] TED website: www.ted.com

[65] TED website: www.ted.com

[66] Martela, F. and Ryan, R. M. (2016). 'Prosocial behavior increases well-being and vitality even without contact with the beneficiary: Causal and behavioural evidence'. *Motivation and Emotion*, 40, 351–357. https://doi.org/10.1007/s11031-016-9552-z

[67] Brown, S. L., Nesse, R. M., Vinokur, A. D., and Smith, D. M. (2003). 'Providing social support may be more beneficial than receiving it: Results from a prospective study of mortality'. *Psychological Science*, 14(4), 320–327. https://doi.org/10.1111%2F1467-9280.14461

[68] Lean In website: https://leanin.org

[69] Action for Happiness website: https://actionforhappiness.org

[70] BBC (2019). 'Dunbar's number: Why we can only maintain 150 relationships'. Available from www.bbc.com/future/article/20191001-dunbars-number-why-we-can-only-maintain-150-relationships [accessed 12 May 2022].

71 Gabrielle Roth's 5Rhythms website: www.5rhythms.com/gabrielle-roths-5rhythms/

72 Nia website: https://nianow.com

73 21 Gratitudes: Movement Medicine Online website: https://21gratitudes.com

74 Biodanza website: www.biodanza.org/en/home-5/

75 Li, Q. (2018). "'Forest bathing" is great for your health. Here's how to do it'. *TIME*, 1 May 2018. Available from https://time.com/5259602/japanese-forest-bathing/ [accessed 12 May 2022].

76 Ferrucci, P. (2000). *What We May Be: The Vision and Techniques of Psychosynthesis*, Tarcher/Putnam.

77 Oliver, T. (2020). *The Self Delusion: The Surprising Science of Our Connection to Each Other and the Natural World*, Weidenfeld & Nicolson.

78 Roger, C. R. (1995). *On Becoming a Person: A Therapist's View of Psychotherapy*, 2nd ed., Houghton Mifflin.

79 Feldman Barrett, L. (2020). *Seven and a Half Lessons about the Brain*, Picador.

Index